A Short History of

QUEER
WOMEN

A Short History of

QUEER WOMEN

KIRSTY LOEHR

ONEWORLD

A Oneworld Book

First published by Oneworld Publications in 2022
Reprinted three times in 2023

ISBN 978-0-86154-284-0
eISBN 978-0-86154-285-7

Typeset by Tetragon, London
Printed and bound in Great Britain by Clays Ltd, Elcograf S.p.A.

Oneworld Publications
10 Bloomsbury Street
London WC1B 3SR
England

For all the queers mentioned in this book and all the queers who remain hidden in history. Without you lot, I wouldn't have the freedom that I have now, this book would never have been written, and my son would probably never have been born.

Oh, and for my cats, Max, Marmaduke and Mitchell (and my beloved Eric). Because what's a lesbian without her cats?

CONTENTS

AUTHOR'S NOTE

This is a revisionist history that the reader too can revise.

As this is a history book, I am dealing with people who are no longer alive and cannot tell us how they identify. There are many reasons women in the past opted out of womanhood – some would certainly have been trans, others were simply trying to live and love as best they could. But to avoid superimposing my own beliefs – and for utmost narrative clarity – I choose to refer to them how history has generally referred to them: by their birth sex. And, as we know, the past is not always indicative of the future, so please feel free to get out your red pen and edit the pronouns as you see fit and according to your understanding of them. My intention is for this book to be an open and inclusive conversation.

SOMEONE, I SAY, WILL REMEMBER US

It is said that the poet Sappho invented the lesbian sometime between *c.*620 and 570 BCE. Men had been screwing each other for a while by then. We know this is true because it had been written about (by men), sung about (by men) and encouraged (by women repulsed by men).

Since then, historians have pretended that Sappho was just *fond* of her students in a totally non-sexual way. Sure, she may have written over ten thousand lines of dazzling verse about same-sex attraction, but that doesn't prove anything, does it?

So the lesbian disappeared and didn't re-emerge until Ellen DeGeneres said, 'Yep, I'm gay' on the cover of *TIME* magazine in 1997. Ellen explained that there were more of her kind and that they looked just like everybody else but because she was a comedian, the Western world thought she was joking. As it became clear this wasn't a joke, they killed her… career.

That is the history of lesbianism. The end.

()

Of course it isn't! These are just a couple of examples in a vast fish stew. And are we really supposed to believe that women weren't fooling around with one another before Sappho got her fingers wet?

Female same-sex desire has been written out of history since, well, forever. If queer women *did* exist, it was because:

A) Men found them attractive, which benefited the patriarchy in some way.

B) …

My theory goes as follows. Before Sappho, before literacy, life was quite simple. Back then, a long time ago, a really long time ago, between forty thousand and fourteen thousand years ago, everybody was shagging everybody, all holes were goals, and days were spent drawing pictures in caves. The concept of fidelity, identity, sexuality and gender were non-existent, and, best of all, nobody gave a toss.

Sometime later, let's say around 9000 BCE, things changed. Days were spent constructing homes, farming and forging stable relationships. There were men, there were women, there were penises and there were vaginas. But still, nobody minded who went with who and what went with what. They were quite happy to just get on with it. Men and women were equal, it was a solid 26°C from June through to September,[1] and nobody had to unstack the dishwasher.

One day, around 3200 BCE, someone, probably a woman, invented a writing system that evolved into several different languages all over the world. Not long after that, a man used this literary development to write a letter to a male friend. In that letter, he joked that women were bad writers, especially when compared to men. It probably went something like this...

Knock Knock.

Who's there?

A female writer.

Yeah right!

[Both men laugh uncontrollably]

It was the first joke ever told at women's expense and everybody thought it was hilarious. The joke was retold so many times that people began mistaking fiction for fact.

---

1 Sure, this may not 'technically' be true, but I think we can all agree that 26°C is the perfect temperature. Don't come at me.

Realising the power of the written word, this man started making more jokes about women being stupid and physically incapable of doing *important things*, like hunting for food, building houses, providing for their family, opening jam jars, playing football, drinking pints of lager, and driving. Some of this might have happened a bit later, but you get it.

A couple of years later, the same man happened to walk in on one of his lady lovers having sex with another woman. Because everybody was sleeping together, he didn't care. But as he was about to leave, something caught his eye. He had never before seen a woman make those facial expressions... or heard those noises.

The man quickly penned another letter to his man friend telling him that women sleeping with one another was dangerous and that they should be stopped. He added that maybe men should stop sleeping with each other too, but that they could work that bit out later. The letter probably looked something like this:

Ides of May, 3150 BCE

Dear Rylan,
How are you doing? Just a thought, do you think that women should stop having sex with each other? It doesn't include us, and

I'm worried they might like it better. Maybe we should stop having sex too. But only if you want to.

Say hi to your mum!

Kev x

The letter went viral and attitudes towards women doing it with one another instantly changed because it threatened a newly formed social system: THE PATRIARCHY.

For instance, in Ancient China, women were only allowed to take part in *tui-shih* (eating each other) or *mojingzi* (rubbing mirrors) if they showed the same affection to their husbands who now *owned* them. That escalated quickly.

But there was *Jinglanhui* (the Golden Orchid Society, 1644–1949 CE), a place where women could go to avoid marrying men. Because the women were mostly (and obviously) all lesbians, the relationships were sexual, and when one of them wanted to marry another one they would ask by offering them a nut, followed by, 'Hi, can I cashew a question?' OK, it was a peanut but I take what I can!

The wedding would be followed by a massive female-only party. The newly married couple could even adopt a daughter if they liked. For a while, everybody thought it was rather nice, but then the patriarchy caught wind of this dreamlike utopia and swiftly banned it.

In Baghdad, the ʿAbbāsid caliph al-Hādī (764–786 CE) had heard rumours that two women in his harem were getting it on *without* him. Furious, he sent two spies to catch them in the act, which they did. To make a point, al-Hādī had them beheaded. To make an even bigger point, he decorated their heads and presented them to the court as a warning.

Finally, in central Africa during the first half of the eighteenth century, the Zande men were worried. Apparently, their wives were so desperate for sex that they had started screwing each other when their husbands were off doing *important things*. One man said, 'Wives would cut a sweet potato or manioc root in the shape of the male organ, or use a banana for the purpose. Two of them would shut themselves in a hut and one would lie on the bed and play the female role while the other, with the artificial organ tied round her stomach, played the male role. They then reversed roles.'

So that's where that came from.

The Zande men admitted that once a woman had been with another woman it was difficult for them to stop doing it, especially because they weren't able to get the same amount of pleasure from their husbands. Sounds about right?

Female same-sex desire was eventually deemed abnormal, immoral, perplexing and, worst of all, gross. It soon became easier to pretend it never existed and inventing history became another beloved pastime of the patriarchy.

But I'm getting ahead of myself. Let's go back to 630 BCE: men were in charge, and women were feeble little creatures who could only manage minor tasks like getting through day two of their period without killing anyone, and pushing small humans out of their vaginas.

Over in Athens, women were regarded as irrational idiots, desperate to get laid! When they weren't trying to get laid, they were being hysterical on account of having a uterus, which is just basic science so no complaints here.

Women were not allowed to leave the house and usually had to stay in a room near the enslaved people's quarters.

Thankfully, things were a bit more relaxed on Lesbos, a small Greek island located in the Aegean Sea. While women were still treated like absolute dog shit, they could at least leave their houses and, if they were really lucky, they could write.

Sappho and the birth of the *lesbian*

One such woman was Sappho, a singer-songwriter who wrote around ten thousand lines of verse. Beat that, Allen Ginsberg. Sappho enjoyed writing about erotic love, an erotic love she felt for her own sex. She recited these poems while playing the lyre, a stringed harp-like instrument that required long fingernails. Because long fingernails were counter-productive to Sappho's personal life, she invented the plectrum and cut her nails short. Lesbian inge-nuity at its finest!

At first, everybody was like, *wow, this poetry is so fresh and exciting*, but then the patriarchy remembered that this kind of love could be damaging, so they exiled her. And they say women over-react!

· The people of Lesbos were like, 'Hey, where has Sappho gone?'

The patriarchy was like, 'Oh… she left for polit-ical reasons.'

The people of Lesbos: 'Really? What political reasons?'

The patriarchy: 'Oh, no, sorry, we meant to say that she fell in love with a boatman and left town.'

The people of Lesbos: 'That doesn't sound like Sappho? Especially considering she's been shagging half the women on the island.'

The patriarchy: 'Yeah, crazy, isn't it? I guess it just goes to show that she was waiting for the right man to come along.'

The people of Lesbos: 'OK, can we at least have her address so we can let her know how well her poetry is doing?'

The patriarchy: 'Oh… hmmm. No, she jumped off the Leucadian cliffs and she's dead now, sorry.'

To make matters worse, it has been suggested that, years later, early Christian Church authorities arranged for all Sappho's work to be destroyed. Thankfully, some was salvaged, though to this day, it is regarded as one of the greatest losses to the literary canon.

()

The Ancient Greeks loved writing and telling stories, and while many of these stories were mythological, they also contained some truth. Therefore, it is easy to understand why so many historians have had trouble figuring out what was real and what was absolute nonsense. One example of this can be found in the story of the Amazons.

In Greek mythology, the Amazons were the daughters of Ares, the god of war. The story goes that the Amazons navigated a female-only society. To continue their bloodline, they would visit a nearby tribe, use the men to breed, then make a quick exit in the morning. So, who did the Amazons bone for pleasure? Each other of course!

No one knew why they were called the Amazons, but one Ancient Greek theory was linked to the words *a-mazos* (without a breast). The idea was one breast was cut or 'burnt' off (I didn't know they melted but, again, science), allowing for safer, more skilful archery. If only they'd known a woman can release an arrow from a bow without chopping her tit off – what a senseless waste of boob!

So yes, the Amazons *did* exist, and they did so with two boobs. And yes, maybe it is a little difficult for historians to fully comprehend what the hell went on in the past, especially when you've got the Ancient Greeks inventing their reality in real time. But when there is actual testimony that points to one woman's erotic attraction for another woman, as in the case of Sappho, it can be frustrating when this is continuously discredited, straightwashed and ignored. And when I say frustrating, I mean *really fucking annoying*.

Speaking of which, many historians also like to say that Sappho couldn't have been a lesbian because 'lesbianism' as a concept did not exist during her time. But then neither did 'straightness', so we're back where we started.

Sappho can be whatever you want her to be.

Sure, she didn't have the vocabulary to 'identify as' lesbian, bisexual, or even queer, but the life she led pre-dates modern terminology and it's circular reasoning at best to discount her orientation and experiences. It's confusing to try to superimpose gender theory, as it's taught today, on a society that didn't operate as such. Also, I can't be arsed.

Some historians, however, are well and truly arsed. In fact, conservative historians are so bothered that they continue to create heterosexual versions of Sappho in the hope that they can distance her from all things lesbian. Their interpretations have had what I imagine are unintended effects, namely, Sappho got even hotter!

Who was Sappho?

1 Sappho was the most heterosexual person on the planet. (conservative historians)
   We love a challenge. (queer women)

2 Sappho was a loving wife to her husband and a loving mother to her children. (conservative historians)
   See above. (queer women)

3 Sappho was the leader of an erotic women's group. (conservative historians)
   Sign us up! (queer women)

4   Sappho was the headmistress of a girls' school. (conservative historians)
    Powerful woman and the owner of her own business, sexy. (queer women)

5   Sappho's most erotic poem about boning women was actually about having a nap. (conservative historians)
    Naps are just as important as queer visibility. (queer women)

6   Sappho was a whore. (patriarchal historians)
    So maybe we would have stood a chance! (queer women)

Sappho's appearance is also hotly debated. No reliable sources exist, but because men have been rating women's looks for centuries, we do have some, admittedly not very helpful, information. One guy described her as beautiful and small, another guy said she was ugly and small, and a different guy said that she had a lovely smile. He was *that* guy, going around Lesbos telling women they should smile more.

One thing we do know for sure is that Sappho's name spawned *sapphist*, a term initially used to describe women who fancied other women. We also know that the word *lesbian* came from Sappho's place of birth, the Isle of Lesbos, thus making Sappho the 'OG' lesbian of Lesbos. Although at one point, *lesbian* also referred to a type of wine... ahh, grape minds think alike!

FORGIVE ME, FOR I HAVE SINNED

When the Roman Empire came along, the patriarchy was in full swing, much like the meat between their legs. The Romans were all about breeding. But no matter how hard two women rubbed, they just couldn't make a baby. So, a lack of reproduction was added to the already colossal list of why women loving women was bad.

Roman men were still allowed to poke each other. They loved it so much that they created lots of different identities to categorise givers and receivers. The Romans didn't need terms for women's sexual preferences because what women prefer was irrelevant to the political agenda then as now.

In 79 CE, in Pompeii, two girls, let's call them Antonia and Fabia, were knee-deep in cunnilingus.

Suddenly, an earthquake struck, but Antonia thought that the resulting trembles were the magnificent skills of Fabia rather than the quakes that had frequently struck the area. The tremor was relatively small, so they went back to having sex before falling asleep in each other's arms.

A few days later, while looking up at the mighty volcano Vesuvius, Antonia decided to show her love for Fabia by scribbling a piece of graffito upon the wall. The next day, the volcano erupted, and Antonia and Fabia were dead, as were all the inhabitants of the surrounding area. The city of Pompeii was discovered centuries later under layers of ash, along with the words, 'I wish I could hold to my neck and embrace the little arms, and bear kisses on the tender lips. Go on, doll, and trust your joys to the winds; believe me, light is the nature of men.'

Only a woman in love with another woman could ever write such schmaltz.

A few decades later, a young Roman poet named Catullus was hanging out in his local library. Catullus loved history, especially the Ancient Greeks, so he picked up a book about it and began to read. As he skimmed through the pages, something caught his eye: an old and fragmented poem that looked like it had been taken from somewhere else and placed inside the pages of the book. Because he was a kleptomaniac, he stuffed the poem into his tunic, and took it home to his girlfriend, Clodia.

'Where did you find this?' Clodia said, shocked.

'It was in the library. Why, what does it say?' Catullus responded.

The poem was in Aeolic Greek, also known as Lesbian dialect, which Clodia just so happened to understand. She looked at Catullus, speechless, then took the poem into the bathroom where she remained for a *very* long time.

From then on, whenever they got down and dirty beneath the sheets Clodia would perform the poem out loud, much to the annoyance of Catullus who still had no idea what she was saying. After another loud and thunderous recital, Catullus snatched the poem out of Clodia's hand and took it to his friend Marcus, who also just so happened to read Aeolic Greek.

'Sappho!' Marcus said, dropping the poem to the floor.

'What is a Sappho?' Catullus said, confused.

'They say there are women like that in Lesbos, masculine-looking, but they don't want to give it up for men. Instead, they consort with women,' Marcus whispered.

'There can't be, I won't believe it!' Catullus said.

'It is true,' Marcus replied, 'I've seen it with my own eyes…'

Roman men, like Catullus and Marcus, could not understand why, or even how, two women had sex without a penis. To try to make sense of it all, the Romans finally attempted to explain *what* these women did in the bedroom, such as rubbing each other aggressively, using dildos and having dangerous, violent sex. They all sound fantastic, but the Romans settled on the Greek word *tribein*, meaning to rub, which then evolved into *tribade* (a woman who rubs her vulva against another woman for sexual pleasure) to help identify them in case they tried to take over the world or something. So, there we have it, yay, we have a name!

Oh, and then came the Christians.

Does religion make the world a better place?

The Christians hated tribades, but they also hated men doing it with one another. They asked the Romans to stop, but the Romans weren't keen on the idea and asked the Christians to rethink their proposal. The Christians were like, 'If a man also lie with mankind, as he lieth with a woman, both of them have committed an abomination: they shall surely be put to death; their blood shall be upon them.'

The answer was no.

While the Christians didn't like any same-sex relationships, it was female same-sex relationships that really rankled. Paul the Apostle, known to his die-hard fans as Saint Paul, thought that it went against nature, whatever that is, and that they should be punished in hell, wherever that is.

Judaism also didn't like it. However, there was one tiny glimmer of hope for Jewish queer women, that of Ruth and her mother-in-law Naomi. And no, this is not the plotline of a cheap porno, but quite an important part of the Hebrew Bible.

In the Book of Ruth, Ruth tells her mother-in-law that she will follow her wherever she goes and wherever she lodges and that her people will be her people and her god will be her god. Sounds a bit like a marriage vow to me…

By then, both of their husbands were dead so Ruth could have just left and found a new husband if she wanted to. But she doesn't leave. She chooses to hang out with her mother-in-law in a world where women didn't really make individual choices. Tremendous!

It was clear that most religions had no room for same-sex desire. For instance, in the Quran, same-sex desire is mentioned at least five times but, spoiler alert, not in a good way. Interestingly, Arabic terms for women loving other women (*sahq*, *sihaq* and *sihaqa*) stemmed from the verbs 'to grind' or 'to pound', you know, like pesto, guacamole, or vagina. It was clear that, according to most religions, same-sex desire was still more about actions than identities.

One Andalusian woman who enjoyed pounding the pesto was the princess of Córdoba, Wallada bint-al-Mustakfi (994/1011–1091). Wallada wore see-through fabrics, and set up her own female literary salon. She was also open about her love affairs and wasn't afraid to let the people of Córdoba know that she was banging both men and women. The inhabitants of Córdoba were ruffled. To ruffle them even more, Wallada wrote about her sexual escapades and stitched them into her tunic – in gold! So everyone in town could read all about them.

Islamic philosophers and physicians also had a lot to say. One guy, al-Kindī, said that women were lesbians because they had itchy vaginas. Another guy, Yuhanna ibn Masawaih, agreed, helpfully adding that if a pregnant woman eats celery, her daughter will end up fancying women. Hence the 'all lesbians are vegans' trope.

In the *Vinaya*, a rule book for Buddhists, there are many references to nuns shagging one another, as well as monks. However, Buddhism also has the word *pandaka*, a term that has a wide range of meanings, and when I say wide, I mean basically everything that is not an able-bodied straight man. This can be anything from gays, bisexuals, impotent men, intersex people, voyeurs, and, of course, people who are sexually aroused in parallel with the stages of the moon. We can't forget them, can we?

The Aztecs also used the word 'hermaphrodite' (*patlācheh*) to describe female same-sex relations which then eventually evolved into what would now be referred to as a lesbian. *Patlācheh* was also used to describe women who carried out 'masculine activities' like chopping wood, building fires and boning women.

Meanwhile, Hindu gods often flirted with gender fluidity. There are also many references to woman-on-woman sex that have appeared in Hindu literature, art and even religious scripts. How refreshing! However, some Sanskrit texts claim that women who love other women are actually conceived when men and women have sex in the cowgirl position. Again, if a woman has any agency, unnatural things *will* happen.

()

When the Roman Empire eventually tumbled around 476 CE, Christianity was rampant. Even though it was mostly men who had issues with female same-sex desire, several women were disgusted by it too, and continued being disgusted by it for hundreds and hundreds of years.

One of these women was the German writer Saint (!) Hildegard of Bingen (1098–1179).

Hildegard suffered from excruciating migraines, often served with a side of hallucinations. As these were *obviously* messages from God, Hildegard made sure to draw them all in a book she called *Scivias*. Many of Hildegard's illustrations resembled giant vulvas, even though she was absolutely adamant that they weren't. Know the ways of the Lord, indeed!

Hildegard was also in love with her female friend Richardis von Stade. Richardis had been helping Hildegard with her book, among other things, and remained a very close confidante throughout her life. Nevertheless, despite routinely drawing vaginas and being obviously very much in love with a woman, Hildegard hated anything to do with tribades, especially when they wore men's clothes.

Hildegard was all like, 'A woman who takes up devilish ways and plays a male role in coupling with another woman is most vile in My sight...' Blah blah blah, Hildegard, go back to drawing massive vulvas, will you?

Thankfully, not all women were repressed lesbians because a century or so later, around 1350, a noblewoman, let's call her Maud de Claud, some-how managed to create her very own midwife mas-turbation association.

It all started when Maud complained to her doctor about her painful pelvis. The doctor declared that her womb had been suffocated due to zero penis action which had resulted in a build-up of seed. Maud hadn't been near her husband's dick in years, so the doctor asked if he could poke his penis inside her to release the seed. Maud asked if the midwife could do it instead. The doctor agreed and the midwife gave Maud an orgasm after plac-ing several hot items, on, around and inside her vagina. Genius.

Maud told all her friends, who immediately complained to their doctors about a mysterious build-up of seed in their wombs, and that it really should be released by a midwife. It didn't take long for the Christians to figure out what was going on, and as soon as they did, they outlawed the midwife practice and warned women that masturbation (by themselves or by anybody else) would result in a trip to the flaming pits of hell, or something along those lines; you lose track after a while.

If you can't beat 'em, punish 'em (by beating 'em)

Unfortunately for the Christians, hell wasn't scary enough anymore. So they had to come up with a list of other potential punishments. In France, when a man got caught bumming, he lost his testicles; if he did it again, he lost his penis; if he did it a third time (how?!), he was burned to death. Because the French didn't really understand female bodies, they cheerfully applied the same rules to women.

In the first half of the thirteenth century, Frenchwoman Bietris de Romans was in love with her neighbour Maria. Bietris was very open about her feelings for Maria and wrote extremely romantic poetry to make it even clearer. Luckily for Bietris, her testicles and penis remained intact, in that they never existed.

Also in France, a lady named Laurence was imprisoned for banging her neighbour Jehanne. Laurence, fearing testicle removal, told everyone that she was happily married and that Jehanne had been chasing her since like forever. Jehanne was shocked and hit back, claiming that Laurence was just another bored straight girl looking for excitement. Laurence was eventually freed and went back to her husband, but you know what they say, once you go tribade…

This kind of tomfoolery wasn't limited to France, because as time went on, more and more ludicrous ventures got going, such as witch-hunting, which became popular all over Europe. Yes, women were now being accused of sorcery, heresy and, of course, causing male impotence – I mean, what else would cause that? By the late 1400s, catching witches was so popular that a Catholic handbook named the *Malleus Maleficarum* (The Hammer of Witches) was published. The aim of the book? To help people detect witchcraft and female sexuality. The book also advocated for the extermination of all lesbians – sorry, *witches* – and was a bestseller for almost two hundred years, second only to the Bible. I'm guessing the readerships overlapped.

But even mass extermination couldn't stop lesbians, so in the early seventeenth century, the Presbyterians came up with an idea that if women continued to have sex with each other then they would be banned from the Church for good. 'Oh no!' said nobody.

It didn't stop Scottish lasses Elspeth Faulds and Margaret Armour rolling around half-naked. Despite a distinct lack of penises involved, they were found guilty of sodomy.

For Catholics, plenty of girl-on-girl action was to be had in the cloisters. Take the twenty-year-old Mexican Agustina Ruiz, who was accused of paddling the pink canoe to visions of the Virgin Mary. And how did they know? Apparently Agustina had told the local priest about her late-night finger-painting during confession. The visions were said to have included a few 'dishonest words' with Jesus Christ, and a few sexual positions with the Virgin Mary. I suppose there are worse things to masturbate to.

Also in Mexico, sixteen-year-old Sor Juana Inés de la Cruz (1648–95) asked her parents if she could go to university. Her parents refused because only men were allowed to go to university, so Sor Juana asked if she could go to university disguised as a man. Her parents still said no but suggested that she go to a convent instead, because that's the same.

Once at the convent, Sor Juana became an avid reader and had up to four thousand books in her personal library. Her library became very famous, so much so that Sor Juana turned her convent quarters into a literary salon. *Lesbians love a salon!* The salon was visited by the city's intellectual crème de la crème and even attracted the Countess María Luisa Manrique de Lara y Gonzaga, the vicereine of New Spain.

Sor Juana wrote several saucy poems to María that explicitly detailed their love. Sadly, the relationship ended on a sour note. So the heartbroken Sor Juana responded the only way a lesbian knows how, penning an angsty poem accusing Countess María of using and discarding her. She walked so Tegan and Sara could run.

Many people at the time didn't really like her lesbian-inspired poetry, nor her pro-equality stance. She also criticised the Catholic Church for only allowing men to have leadership positions, which resulted in the Church confiscating her books. Thus neatly proving her point!

LOTHARIOS AND LEATHER DILDOS

Germany, 1477. Katherina Hetzeldorfer was caught using a giant red leather dildo with a woman who was supposed to be her sister. She was really her missus. Not only does Katherina gain queer points for using her imagination so early on, but she also has the glorious (and awful) accolade of being the first woman ever to be convicted and executed for simply fancying women, a crime that didn't actually have a name at this point.

The authorities were more annoyed that Katherina had penetrated another woman with a giant red dildo rather than with her fingers. She was then taken to the river Rhine and drowned. Think about that next time you use a strap-on.

To strap or not to strap?
That is the question

Just like today, dildos were a common accessory among queer women. Only then, they weren't as veiny (what's the *deal* with that??). Italian stallion Catterina Vizzani was known to carry a leather dildo between her legs and used it to bed over one hundred women.

Catterina began her bid for top shagger at just fourteen years old, when she fell in love with her embroidery teacher. The affair lasted for two years, until the embroidery teacher's father caught them in bed. The father threatened to have Catterina arrested so she left town and reinvented herself as Giovanni Bordoni.

Giovanni was just as charming as Catterina, and soon built up a reputation as a serial seducer. That is until she fell in love with the niece of a local minister. Giovanni wanted to marry her, but the minister forbade them from being together due to Giovanni's raunchy reputation. The couple didn't care, and decided to get married in secret without the minister's blessing. Unfortunately for Giovanni, the minister found out before they could be married and shot Giovanni in the leg. In the hospital, minutes from death, Giovanni asked for a nun to come to her bed. She then confessed that she had been born a woman and wished to be buried in women's clothing.

After Catterina/Giovanni's death, a surgeon attempted to find an explanation for what he called 'those who followed the practices of Sappho'.

First, he removed the hymen, then the clitoris, followed by the fallopian tubes, the intestines, the liver and the gallbladder. He then examined them all closely, making sure to use all his expertise and knowledge in the field of biology. And what did he find? Absolutely fuck all.

Colonisation, it's very unsettling

Over in what would later become the United States of America, European colonists were busy making babies while killing the people who had already lived there for centuries.

One colonist, clergyman John Cotton, wanted to draw up a bill that made the 'unnatural filth-iness', that is same-sex sex, punishable by death. Unnatural it's not, filthy if you're lucky. Nobody listened to John Cotton, because the settlers were either infecting the indigenous population with their fatal European diseases or stealing their land and slaughtering them. Nevertheless, Cotton's 'unnatural filthiness' idea started to gather pace.

In Plymouth County, not far from where Cotton lived, the married Sarah White Norman and the also married Mary Vincent Hammon shared their first kiss. From that day forward, the two would sneak kisses whenever they could, kisses that soon escalated into full-blown finger fun in Mary's bedroom.

One morning, after Mary's husband had left the house, Sarah snuck in and joined Mary in her marital bed. The pair quickly got down to business but were discovered by Mary's husband, who had unexpectedly returned. Sarah and Mary were then prosecuted for 'lewd behaviour with each other upon a bed'. Sarah was convicted and told to publicly acknowledge her 'unchaste behaviour', while Mary got away with it because she was the younger of the two. It was OK, though – they just started conducting lewd behaviour with each other on the floor instead.

()

America was becoming home to many immigrants from all over the world. One settler was Irish-born Anne Bonny, who found herself in South Carolina with her father in the early 1700s. Anne was a regular in the local taverns and drank all day and all night. Unfortunately for those around her, she was a terrible drunk who once stabbed a servant girl to death (bad) but also hospitalised a would-be rapist (good).

Anne's father wanted her to settle down with a nice man who lived around the corner. Anne said no and married another man instead. Anne's father was fuming and disinherited her. Anne got drunk and burned down his plantation. The two went back and forth for a while until Anne and her husband ran away to the Caribbean. One of the first things she did when she arrived was shoot a sailor's ear off after he had the audacity to get in her way.

One day, Anne met the notorious pirate John 'Calico Jack' Rackham. The two were quite taken with one another, so much so that Calico Jack asked Anne's husband if he could pay him to divorce her. The husband said no but Anne left her husband anyway and joined Calico Jack at sea. The rest of the crew weren't very happy, because women at sea were seen as bad luck, but Anne being Anne didn't let the hostility bother her, and even stabbed a sneering shipmate to make a point.

While on board, Anne dressed like a pirate, behaved like a pirate and fought like a pirate. She also met the dashing Mark Read, a renowned swashbuckler known for his confident nature and good looks. Mark Read was in fact a woman named Mary, but Anne didn't know that yet.

Mary first began dressing in male clothes after her mother encouraged her to pretend to be her dead brother to claim inheritance. Mary embraced the male attire and decided to wear it full time, but her mother thought she was weird and disowned her. Classic maternal gaslighting.

The story goes that Anne and Mark Read fell in love, each believing the other to be male. Anne then went to Mark's room, flashed him her tit, and revealed that she was actually a woman. Funnily enough, Mark then took out her tit and the two went at it like rabbits. Calico Jack had no idea what was going on but soon became increasingly jealous of Anne and Mark's close relationship. This led to an embarrassing altercation for Calico Jack, who burst into Anne's room to find Mark stretched out on Anne's bed with her boobs out. Calico Jack was shocked, but relieved, as he would rather Anne be with a woman than a pilfering pirate. Wouldn't we all, Jack.

Anne and Mark/Mary Read enjoyed the pirate life and often fought side by side. When Calico Jack's ship was attacked, Anne and Mary were left to take on the attackers themselves while Calico Jack and his men hid below deck. The women were so angry with Calico Jack and his crew that they began shooting at *them* instead.

Boys, this way; girls, that way

Tribades were now running riot all over the world. Not only were they pirates but they were also members of the royal family, like Kristina, the one-time Queen of Sweden (1626–89).

Kristina spent her life disrupting royal narratives. On the day she was born, everybody thought she was a boy because she was hairy and had a big nose. So far, so sexy. When her father (the then king) figured out she was a girl, he declared, 'She'll be clever, she has made fools of us all!'

From an early age, Kristina decided that she did not want to get married, at least not to a man. Kristina was what some people would now call a tomboy, but because that word is silly, let's say she was partial to a pair of trousers and a giant sword. As she grew older, Kristina openly and unashamedly pursued women whom she fancied, such as her handmaiden Ebba Sparre. The pair began a sexual relationship and Kristina started introducing Ebba as her *bedfellow*.[1]

One day, Kristina was bored. Ebba had left court and she had slept with all the other handmaidens. She was also receiving a lot of pressure to marry, so to solve the problem she abdicated the throne.

---

1 A word that I will immediately start using.

Kristina then put on her best male attire, travelled to the Netherlands, and lived the next part of her life chasing Dutch pussy.

Gender-bending existed long before Queen Kristina. However, unlike Kristina, most could not live so freely. One such person was Elena de Céspedes, who was born in 1545 in Granada, Spain. Elena was a victim of descent-based slavery, and when she was eventually freed at sixteen years old, she got married and fell pregnant. Elena's husband died not long into the marriage, and Elena was left with a baby boy. Because it was the sixteenth century, and the sixteenth century hated women (especially Black women), Elena was unable to bring up her son alone, and was forced to leave him with somebody else. She never saw him again.

The birth of Elena's son was so damaging to her that the skin covering the urinary canal was completely broken, revealing the head of what looked like a penis. Elena transformed into Eleno and adopted a masculine lifestyle. She served as a soldier, worked as a tailor, and at one point became a highly respected surgeon. Eleno also began having successful sexual relationships with women such as María del Caño, whom Eleno wanted to marry.

Eleno needed permission to get married so they asked the local priest. The priest was suspicious because Eleno did not have any facial hair. And when a man has no facial hair, he's unable to consummate a marriage, right?

Eleno was then subjected to a horrific and invasive examination which ended in one doctor claiming that Eleno was male – only for another to say that they were actually female. The case went to court, where Eleno was tried by the Spanish inquisition; not a turn of phrase, the *real* Spanish inquisition. In the end, Eleno was given two hundred lashes, marched through the town centre in women's clothes, and sentenced to ten years' confinement in a hospital.

Crap doctors assigning genders according to how they felt on the day (then often changing their mind) was a common occurrence that led to some severe mental health issues. No surprises there. Thankfully, this wasn't always the case; every now and again the individual involved seized the reins of their gender, like Catharina Margaretha Linck.

Catharina lived sometimes as a woman and sometimes as a man. When presenting as a man, she went by the name of Anastasius Lagrantius Rosenstengel, a soldier with a huge dick, or what was actually a homemade leather dildo with two testicles made from a pig's bladder.

In the early 1700s, Anastasius met Catharina Margaretha Mühlhahn. The two got married but the marriage wasn't a happy one. Plus, Catharina Margaretha Mühlhahn kept berating Catharina Margaretha Linck for being unable to urinate properly, and wondered why they kept pissing on their shoes. This is genuinely what happened. They also had the same first and middle name, which is funny!

Alas, Catharina Margaretha Mühlhahn had an annoying and interfering mother. The mother didn't trust Catharina Margaretha Linck (Anastasius), which ultimately led to a massive fight in which she ripped off Catharina Margaretha Linck's clothes and called the authorities. Rude.

The two Catharinas were put on trial for female sodomy. During the trial, Linck was subjected to an unnecessary examination by two medical witnesses who noted 'nothing hermaphroditic, much less masculine'.

Mühlhahn then said she didn't know that Linck had been born female and that 'her genitals had become very swollen and painful from the friction' of the homemade leather strap-on. Linck insisted that Mühlhahn *did* know and not only had she fondled her breasts but that she had also 'frequently held the leather instrument in her hands and had stuck it in her vagina, which she would not have done if it had not felt pleasurable to her'. Then someone passed her a mic to drop.

In the end, it was determined that Satan was actually to blame, and that Catharina Margaretha Linck should be burned alive, but because humanity was becoming less bloodthirsty and more empathetic, it was decided that she would first be beheaded and *then* burned.

Was she a lesbian? Was she bisexual? Was she queer? Was she trans? We can't know the answers to these questions. All we know is she *existed*, like many before and after.

LESBIANS IN HIGH PLACES

In England during the early 1700s, the writer William King was angry. He was adamant that Lady Frances Brudenell (otherwise known as the Countess of Newburgh) owed him some money, so he took her to court. William lost the case, so in revenge, he wrote an epic satirical poem called *The Toast*. The poem portrayed Lady Frances as a wanton witch who also happened to be the leader of a lesbian society. It was the first time the word 'lesbian' was used in reference to female same-sex desire, and, unlike tribade, this one stuck...

William wasn't the only satirist in town. The writer Delarivier Manley (1663/*c*.1670–1724) was also quite the comedian, and routinely parodied politicians across the country. But, unlike William, Delarivier was a woman, which meant she wasn't safe. Arrests and libel threats ensued.

Delarivier Manley was responsible for the lesbian rumours regarding the reigning queen at the time, Queen Anne. Delarivier often targeted Queen Anne's right-hand woman, Sarah Churchill, Duchess of Marlborough, and the romantic relationship between them. This then led to accusations that Queen Anne and Sarah were doing it. Delarivier was correct, they *were* doing it! And there's even a film to prove it!

Queen Anne (Olivia Colman) and Sarah (Rachel Weisz) first met as children. They immediately grew close and even had pet names for one another: Anne was Mrs Morley, and Sarah, Mrs Freeman. As they grew older, they became even closer, and whenever Sarah would leave court, Anne would send her long and soppy love letters detailing how much she was missing her.

When Anne became queen, Sarah held great influence and often guided the Queen on her political decisions. This was all well and good until the arrival of Sarah's cousin, Abigail Hill (Emma Stone). The Queen took a liking to Abigail, and soon Sarah found herself out of favour. Sarah was livid, so she blackmailed Anne and threatened to release all the love letters that Anne had written. Sarah then orchestrated a smear campaign against Abigail, which included a really funny song about how Abigail was a dirty chambermaid who could not write. Unfortunately for Sarah, nothing seemed to work, and Queen Anne just fancied Abigail more.[1]

It all came to an explosive end when Sarah publicly insulted Queen Anne at a church service after Anne had refused to wear the jewels that Sarah had chosen for her. This resulted in Sarah's dismissal from court, and her husband was told to return Sarah's gold key to the royal bedchamber. Not a euphemism. Sarah being Sarah decided to rob a few grand from the privy purse and then remove all the brass locks from every door in the house that she was asked to leave. Honestly, how can anyone think lesbianism is a modern concept when the story of Queen Anne and Sarah Churchill is the quintessential lesbian drama?

()

Queen Anne wasn't the only royal dabbling in the dark arts of lesbianism. Marie Antoinette, Queen of France, was at it too. Marie wasn't exactly beloved by her people; she spent a lot of money, ate a lot of food, and didn't seem too bothered that her subjects were starving in the streets. Although

---

1 Just so you know, even though you never asked, I'm Team Sarah, but I think that might have something to do with the fact that Rachel Weisz played her in the movie.

to be fair, Marie didn't really have a say in the matter, as that was the job of her husband, King Louis XVI.

Marie and Louis were hardly love's young dream, and initially got together to form a political alliance between France and Marie's home country, Austria. The pair were utterly ill-suited. Louis was painfully shy, indecisive and cold. On the other hand, Marie was lavish, outgoing and extremely shallow. They were so uninterested in one another that it took them a whopping seven years to consummate their marriage.

Of course, Marie was to blame for the lack of sex and the noticeable lack of an heir. She only had *one* job, after all. The French media wanted her to know what a rubbish woman she was so they created cartoons about her failing sexual organs and wrote songs about how her body couldn't do what it was supposed to do.

Marie may not have been interested in her husband, but she was most certainly into the ladies, and at one time was caught drooling over English writer Mary Robinson's tits. The incident was later reported in Mary's memoirs: 'She appeared to survey, with peculiar attention, a miniature of the Prince of Wales, which Mrs. Robinson wore on her bosom…'

We've all done it.

But it was the nineteen-year-old widow Marie Thérèse Louise of Savoy who was Marie's personal favourite. Marie was so charmed by Marie Thérèse Louise that she regularly showered her with gifts and made her the superintendent of the royal household, which sounds more like a punishment than anything else.

Marie and Marie Thérèse Louise wrote passionate letters to one another, addressing each one with 'my dear heart' and ending with 'a heart entirely yours'. But, like all horny queens, Marie Antoinette was keeping her options (and her legs) open. Enter Yolande Martine Gabrielle de Polastron.

Yolande was dubbed the most beautiful woman in France. Marie showed her affection by paying Yolande's debts, moving her into a massive apartment in Versailles, and eventually making Yolande's husband a duke and therefore Yolande a duchess. This encouraged the French media to pipe up again, releasing thousands of pamphlets depicting the two in a range of sexual positions.

As we all know, things didn't quite work out for Marie, as she famously met a grisly end with the guillotine during the French Revolution. But, before her death, Marie was allowed one final goodbye with her lover, not Louis XVI, but Marie Thérèse Louise. Marie Thérèse Louise had earlier been arrested and put on trial, where she refused to swear hatred to the King and Queen. She was then taken outside to a baying mob who murdered her. They cut off her head, took it to where Marie was being kept, and demanded that she give her one-time lover a final kiss. Bloody hell, that's unnecessary!

()

Over in Ireland, single lady Eleanor Butler (1739–1829) was embarrassing her upper-class family by refusing to marry. Not far from where Eleanor lived, Sarah Ponsonby, sixteen years her junior, was doing the same thing. One morning, while out on a walk, the pair crossed paths and were instantly drawn to one another. They decided to run away together, move abroad and buy a house. What does a lesbian bring on a second date? A removal van of course! Again, we've all done it.

Because it was the end of the 1700s, it was rather difficult for two women to run away together. On the night of their escape, Sarah had to jump out of her bedroom window while dressed in men's clothing. She also brought her dog, Frisk, because a lesbian cannot skip town without her dog. Also, Frisk! The pair met up in a barn before mounting a couple of horses and galloping several miles to board a ship that would take them to England. Sadly, Eleanor and Sarah were unable to board the ship and were eventually found by their families and taken home.

Eleanor and Sarah were told never to talk to one another again, and Eleanor was threatened with the convent, although we all know what happens in the convent. Eleanor took no notice, ran away and hid in… Sarah's bedroom. It was as effective as when a toddler hides behind a curtain with her toes sticking out. But the families were over it and agreed that the lovers could go, but that they could never return to the family home. Result!

The women settled in a small, picturesque village named Llangollen, in north Wales. The locals soon referred to Eleanor and Sarah as the 'Ladies of Llangollen' because they were ladies, and they lived in Llangollen. Original, right? By contrast, Eleanor and Sarah excelled in imagination; they redesigned their cottage in trendy gothic chic, studied literature and learnt several languages. They also devoted their time to hosting friends and curious visitors who had never seen real-life lesbians before. The ladies attracted all sorts of interesting people, from Mary Shelley's husband Percy, the mad, bad and dangerous to know Lord Byron, and even the Duke of Wellington.

Eleanor and Sarah lived together for over fifty years. When they died the people of Llangollen were unhappy with the lesbian reputation that their quaint little village had acquired, so it was decided that from then on, they would tell people that the Ladies of Llangollen were simply good friends. They were friends who shared a bed, friends who had sex, friends who called each other 'my beloved' and 'my better half' and friends with other friends called Molly the Bruiser.[2]

The lesbian player makes an appearance

Another person who visited the Ladies of Llangollen was the West Yorkshire-born iconic lesbian player Anne Lister (1791–1840). The lesbian player is well known around the gay community, and is easy to identify. She usually comes in the shape of a well-dressed, arrogant arsehole, with a charming nickname. She is smart, funny, excellent in bed, coupled with severe parental issues, a fear of commitment and a strange sense of vulnerability that is so incredibly narcissistic yet implausibly attractive, especially with a pint in one hand.

Anne's nickname was 'Gentleman Jack' due to her masculine dress and love for the ladies.

2　Every lesbian has a Molly the Bruiser in her life. If you don't have one, then it's probably you.

She was also an extraordinarily successful (and rather privileged) landowner who wasn't afraid to take on the also successful (and rather privileged) male landowners in the area. Although the name 'Gentleman Jack' was initially deemed as an insult, it has, to some extent, been reclaimed, much in the same way as dyke or queer.

Anne's womanising ways began at just thirteen years old, when she met Eliza Raine. The two ended up sharing a room at boarding school, and we all know what happens in boarding school. Anne soon broke Eliza's heart after getting off with a couple of her classmates. At the time, it was common practice for lovers to exchange a snippet of pubic hair. Anne was so successful with the ladies that she had a whole cabinet full of bush.

Anne lived in the extravagant Shibden Hall, which she eventually inherited in 1836. The house was the ultimate shagpad, perfect for Anne's conquests. However, after one too many women, trips abroad and mountains climbed, Anne wanted a wife. The woman in question was Ann Walker, Anne's wealthy but painfully shy neighbour, and yet another example of a lesbian sharing a name with her lover. After a lot of graft, Anne managed to charm the introverted Ann, and in 1834 they exchanged vows and gave each other rings. They also took communion together at the Holy Trinity Church, in York, to confirm their marriage. The church now displays a commemorative rainbow plaque which dubs their nuptials the first-ever lesbian wedding.

We have Anne Lister's diaries to thank for this little slice of history. She started her first diary at fifteen years old and documented just about everything that ever happened in her life, including sexual encounters that were written in code.

The diaries included several tips and tactics on how to seduce women. For instance, when Anne wanted to suss if a lady was into the puss, she would ask them if they were familiar with the scandalous works of Lord Byron, and could tell from their reaction. He was the Sarah Waters of his day. It might have been a clunky flirting technique, but it worked, and it shows us that Anne was trying to understand her sexuality as an identity. See! Lesbians did exist in the past, and guess what? You could even find them outside of West Yorkshire!

Take the working-class hero Wu Zao (1799–1862), a Chinese writer, musician, painter and all-around badass, who somehow managed to learn to read and write in a time when women from lower classes had no access to education.

Wu's work was mostly about female roles in society and how to break away from them. One of her pieces was an opera (yes, she wrote operas too), which included a woman who cross-dressed and complained about gender roles. An opera that would seem quite relevant in any given century. Like Anne Lister, Wu had several relationships, affairs, lovers and associations throughout her life, ranging from mistresses to sex workers and courtesans.

Surprisingly, all the poets and scholars of the time loved it; so much so, they started singing her songs and poems all over China. Then, after people figured out what the songs and poems were *really* about, they stopped, and Wu Zao was buried beneath a cold slab of heteronormativity and never spoken of again.

So yes, lesbians all over the world were carving out identities for themselves through work, creativity and love. How wonderful!

'If I had but been a man, thou wouldst have been the very ticket for me as a wife.'

Charlotte Brontë to 'friend' Ellen Nussey

Only a few miles away from Anne Lister, the legendary novelist Charlotte Brontë (1816–55) had fallen in love with Ellen Nussey. Charlotte first met Ellen at school. Not only was their love immediate but it lasted a whopping twenty-four years accompanied by five hundred love letters. The two were so in love that at one point, Charlotte even considered marrying Ellen's brother Henry, just so she and Ellen could live in the same house. But Henry was too dull, even as a beard.

At the time, women were encouraged to seek intimate relationships with each other. Don't get excited, this was just practice before hitching a permanent ride on a penis. So the internal lives of women like Charlotte and Ellen were overlooked, even when they wrote things like this: 'I am afraid of caring too much for you…'; and, 'If I had but been a man, thou wouldst have been the very ticket for me as a wife…'; oh, and, 'You ought first to be tenderly kissed, and then afterwards as tenderly whipped…'; and, 'Ellen, I wish I could live with you always. I begin to cling to you more fondly than ever I did. If we had but a cottage and a competency of our own, I do think we might live and love on till Death without being dependent on any third person for happiness…'; and, finally, 'Less than ever can I taste or know pleasure till this work is wound up. And yet I often sit up in bed at night, thinking of and wishing for you…'

I feel 'overlooked' is too weak a word in this context. Let's go with 'buried'.

Charlotte turned down the proposals of several men since she was in love with Ellen. But, because this was the beginning of the Victorian age, and the Victorian age hated women, like those other ages,

Charlotte had to marry as it would help support her ageing father. God damn you, patriarchy!

Ellen was devastated by this – breaking off correspondence with Charlotte for the first time. She even tried to enlist the help of a mutual friend, who basically told her to get over it and let Charlotte do her thing. Charlotte *did* marry and remained so for a *whole year* until her death in 1855.

Ellen spent much of her remaining life keeping the memory of Charlotte Brontë alive. Many historians didn't like Ellen's interference in the story of a British literary legend and decided to remove all traces of her.

Over the years it has been speculated that Charlotte Brontë and Anne Lister may have known one another, especially when you look at Charlotte's novel *Shirley*, which tells the story of a female Yorkshire landowner with a penchant for the ladies. And, between 1838 and 1839, Charlotte's sister and fellow novelist Emily lived within minutes of Shibden Hall. By then, Anne and Ann would have been married for a few years, which, as we all know, equals a few centuries in lesbian years.

Sadly, in 1840, at just forty-nine years old, Anne died while travelling in Georgia in the Caucasus. Ann had Anne's body embalmed and shipped back to England so she could be buried in the same church as her aunt and uncle. Now that's love.

Anne's diaries remained hidden until they were found in the mid-1890s by the last inhabitant of Shibden Hall, John Lister. John struggled to decipher the code, so he asked his mate, Arthur Burrell, to help. The pair managed to crack the code, but upon realising what they had found, Arthur advised John to burn them. Thankfully, John didn't take his advice and instead of burning the diaries, he hid them behind a panel at Shibden Hall.

The diaries were eventually found again, and in the 1980s they were deciphered by the writer Helena Whitbread, who would publish the material for the whole world to see. People claimed the diaries were fake because lesbians didn't exist in the past, and if they did, they wouldn't write about love, and… sex, would they? Yes, of course they bloody would. Lesbians love to fall in love. It's a lesbian's favourite thing to do, up there with calling your pets your kids, going on some kind of walking activity, and drawing a moustache on your face when drunk. Lesbians also love to have sex. And guess what? They had sex *then* and they have sex *now*, although swapping snippets of pubic hair seems to have passed its sell-by date, unless I'm missing out on something…

HERE, THERE AND EVERYWHERE

One day, in 1918, Eleanor Roosevelt was unpacking her husband's suitcase and found some saucy love letters hidden under a washcloth. The letters probably looked something like this:

Dear Franklin,
    You're well sexy. I've never Roosefelt this way before.
    Love,
        Lucy Mercer (your social secretary).

Eleanor and Franklin had never really been passionate. In fact, Eleanor hated having sex with Franklin, and once told her daughter it was 'an ordeal to be borne' – an odd thing to tell your daughter, but who am I to judge?

The discovery resulted in Eleanor offering Franklin a divorce. However, a divorce would mark the end of Franklin's political career, so the pair remained married, although Eleanor most definitely had leverage. In front of the cameras, she was the supportive and loyal wife to a future president. Behind closed doors, she had her own interests, such as field hockey, flying with Amelia Earhart, working for the Navy-Marine Corps Relief Society, and joining the Women's Trade Union League. You see where I'm going with this…

Although Eleanor had been born into wealth and privilege, she had an unhappy childhood. By the time she was ten years old, both Eleanor's parents had died, and she had to be protected from some dodgy and perverted uncles. At the age of fifteen she was then sent to the Allenswood Boarding Academy in London, which had an enormously positive effect on her life, mainly because it was run by the lesbian Mademoiselle Marie Souvestre.

Mademoiselle Marie Souvestre was that teacher that all the closeted lesbo kids wanted to bang. She was beautiful, captivating, intelligent and a feminist. She also encouraged her students to think for themselves, something that Eleanor immediately took on board.

Sadly, after a couple of years at Allenswood, Eleanor was summoned back home to New York so she could make her social debut. Not long after, she ran into her fifth cousin (once removed), Franklin Delano Roosevelt, on a train. The rest, as they say, is heteronormative history.

New York was a thrilling place at the time, with a melange of socialites, theatre darlings and political figures all rubbing… shoulders. The city's population had also exploded, with Black people migrating from the segregated South, and the newly opened Grand Central Terminal allowing folk to move between cities much more easily. To be more specific, *lesbians* could move between cities much more easily.

The sewing circle

In the 1920s, the term 'the sewing circle' was used to describe the ever-expanding, underground lesbian scene in the United States. The New York sewing circle was hijacked by the writer and serial woman-iser Mercedes de Acosta, who probably slept with every single woman, straight or otherwise, on the east coast. Mercedes made her way to Hollywood to start a career in the movie industry, and of course, meet some ladies. Once there, Mercedes ended up bedding almost half the women in Hollywood and often boasted, 'I can get any woman away from any man.' Fighting words, of course, but Mercedes was Anne Lister on steroids.

It didn't take long for Mercedes to infiltrate the Hollywood sewing circle, which included the likes of Katharine Hepburn, Judy Garland, Joan Crawford, Hattie McDaniel, Barbara Stanwyck, Tallulah Bankhead and the stunning Swedish recluse Greta Garbo.

Mercedes was immediately taken with Greta, and quickly disintegrated into a fumbling mess. Astonishingly, Mercedes somehow managed to bag the elusive actress, and the pair embarked on a volatile relationship that Greta undoubtedly controlled.

Mercedes was all, 'I love you.'

Greta was like, 'I want to be alone.'

Greta eventually broke Mercedes's heart. It was OK, though, because around the same time, German actress and bisexual bombshell Marlene Dietrich was waiting in the wings. Marlene was a renowned lady-killer. Before making a move on Mercedes, Marlene had been involved with Greta. Greta was so screwed up after the relationship that she pretended never to have even met Marlene.

Marlene liked Mercedes and Mercedes liked Marlene. The pair became serious and even walked their dogs together. Despite such commitment, Marlene and Mercedes never made it official.

Mercedes was still in love with Greta, and remained so for the rest of her life. Marlene was also busy shagging the actress Tallulah Bankhead.

Tallulah Bankhead, who once introduced herself by saying, 'Hello, I'm a lesbian, what do you do?', was not afraid to showcase her sexuality. She once claimed she had bedded over five thousand people, with Greta Garbo, Marlene Dietrich and Hattie McDaniel among them. She was also friends with Eleanor Roosevelt, although they weren't romantically involved, and besides, Eleanor Roosevelt had her hands full with the whiskey-drinking, cigar-smoking, flannel-shirt-wearing Lorena 'Hick' Hickok.

Lesbians in the White House

Hick was the kind of lesbian who probably rolled her own tampons. She was *that* kind of lesbian. You know, the kind of lesbian who isn't objectified by the patriarchy and lives for herself. She was also a reporter, a job deemed unsuitable for women at the time. She even wrote about sport. The cheek!

In 1928, Hick was given the opportunity to interview Eleanor Roosevelt. She obviously enjoyed her time with Eleanor, because not long after the interview she convinced her editor to let her cover Eleanor (wink wink) during Franklin's first presidential campaign. The two quickly struck up a friendship which eventually turned into a romance, and by 1932, they were spending almost every day together. Eleanor even wore a sapphire ring given to her by Hick during Franklin's presidential inauguration. The gall!

Eleanor and Hick sent thousands of ridiculously passionate letters to each other throughout their lives. True to form, historians prefer to straightwash the relationship, despite irrefutable evidence of their blazing love. Like their letters...

THE 'I MISS YOU' LETTER. 5 MARCH 1933

Hick, my dearest,
I cannot go to bed to-night without a word to you. I felt a little as though a part of me was leaving to-night, you have grown so much to be a part of my life that it is empty without you even though I'm busy every minute.

THE 'I LOVE YOU' LETTER. 6 MARCH 1933

Hick darling,
Oh! how good it was to hear your voice, it was so inadequate to try & tell you what

it meant, Jimmy was near & I couldn't say 'je t'aime et je t'adore' as I longed to do but always remember that I am saying it & that I go to sleep thinking of you.

THE 'I'VE BEEN THINKING ABOUT HAVING SEX WITH YOU ALL DAY' LETTER. 7 MARCH 1933

Hick darling,
All day I've thought of you... oh! I want to put my arms around you, I ache to hold you close. Your ring is a great comfort, I look at it & think she does love me, or I wouldn't be wearing it!

THE 'I WANT TO KISS YOU' LETTER. 5 DECEMBER 1933

Only eight more days. Twenty-four hours from now it will be only seven more – just a week! I've been trying today to bring back your face – to remember just how *you look. Funny how even the dearest face will fade away in time. Most clearly I remember your eyes, with a kind of teasing smile in them, and the feeling of that soft spot just northeast of the corner of your mouth against my lips. I wonder what we'll do when we meet – what we'll say. Well – I'm rather proud of us, aren't you? I think we've done rather well.*

THE 'I'M JEALOUS, PRETENDING I'M NOT JEALOUS OF YOUR EX-GIRLFRIEND' LETTER. 4 FEBRUARY 1934

I dread the western trip & yet I'll be glad when Ellie can be with you, tho' I'll dread that too just a little, but I know I've got to fit in gradually to your past & with your friends so there won't be closed doors between us later on & some of this we'll do this summer perhaps. I shall feel you are terribly far away & that makes me lonely but if you are happy I can bear that & be happy too. Love is a queer thing, it hurts but it gives one so much more in return!

THE 'I BOUGHT YOUR DOG A PRESENT THUS CONFORMING TO LESBIAN STEREOTYPES' LETTER. 27 DECEMBER 1940

Thanks again, you dear, for all the sweet things you think of and do. And I love you more than

I love anyone else in the world except Prinz – who, by the way, discovered your present to him on the window seat in the library Sunday.

Sadly, in a panic, Hick burned many of the more explicit letters. Gah! Why does someone *always* burn the letters?! Ah yes, not being allowed to live as your true self because of the constant fear of shame and reputational ruin. That'll be it.

Lesbian jazz singers?

Meanwhile, Eleanor's pal Tallulah had struck up a friendship with the singer Billie Holiday. The pair first met at one of Tallulah's notorious drug-fuelled, booze-filled Hollywood parties. By then, Tallulah was already famous, but Billie had yet to become a star. A decade later, Tallulah dropped in to see Billie (now one of the most famous jazz singers in the world) performing on Broadway. Tallulah's visits became a regular occurrence, and she was eventually awarded with her very own special seat. The friendship turned into a relationship made all the more intense by an abundance of drugs.

In 1956, Billie decided to write about the relationship with Tallulah in her autobiography. Out of courtesy, she asked her publisher, Doubleday, to send Tallulah a copy of the manuscript to make sure that she was fine with what had been written. Tallulah was not fine, and wrote back saying, 'Dahlings, if you publish that stuff about me in the Billie Holiday book, I'll sue you for every god-damned cent that Doubleday can make.'

Billie was not impressed, and responded with one of the best letters in epistolary history.

Dear Miss Bankhead:

I thought I was a friend of yours. That's why there's nothing in my book that was unfriendly to you, unkind or libelous. Because I didn't want to drag you. I tried six times last month to talk to you on the damn phone, and tell you about the book just as a matter of courtesy. That bitch you have who impersonates you kept telling me to call back and when I did it was the same deal until I gave up.

But while I was working out of town, you didn't mind talking to Doubleday and suggesting behind my damn back that I had flipped and/or made up those little mentions of you in my book.

Baby, Cliff Allan and Billy Heywood are still around. My maid who was with me at the Strand isn't dead either. There are plenty of others around who remember how you carried on so you almost got me fired out of the place. And if you want to get shitty, we can make it a big shitty party. We can all get funky together.

I don't know whether you've got one of those damn lawyers telling you what to do or not. But I'm writing this to give you a chance to answer back quick and apologize to me and to Doubleday. Read my book over again. I understand they sent you a duplicate manuscript. There's nothing in it to hurt you. If you think so, let's talk about it like I wanted to last month. It's going to press right now so there is no time for monkeying around.

Straighten up and fly right, Banky. Nobody's trying to drag you.

Billie Holiday.

In the end, Tallulah was only mentioned once as a friend who would sometimes come over to the house to eat spaghetti. Spaghetti?! That's a new one.

WAR, WHAT IS IT GOOD FOR? LESBIANS!

In 1854, just before the American Civil War, domestic worker Addie Brown met Rebecca Primus, the daughter of an important and well-known Connecticut family. The two women were born free, which meant that they never had to undergo the horrors of slavery, though slavery persisted throughout the South.

The two survived the war, and in 1865 Rebecca was asked to leave Connecticut and move south to help build a school for newly freed African Americans. By then, Addie and Rebecca had developed an intense and passionate relationship, so the move was extremely difficult.

Over the next few years, Addie and Rebecca wrote letters detailing their love and lust for one another. In one letter, Addie wrote, 'O my Dear Dear

Rebecca when you press me to your Dear bosom…
happy I was, last night I gave any thing if I could
only layed my poor aching head on your bosom. O
Dear how soon will it be I can be able to do so…'

As time went on, Addie became frustrated. It
had been a long time since she had seen Rebecca,
and she was worried that Rebecca's feelings may
have changed. To find out, Addie played the oldest
trick in the book and attempted to make Rebecca
jealous by suggesting that one of her colleagues
was into her: 'The girls are very friendly towards
me. I am eather in they room or they in mine,
every night out ten and sometimes past. One of
them wants to sleep with me. Perhaps I will give
my consent some of these nights.'[1]

It worked. Rebecca wrote back alarmed and
Addie swiftly backtracked: 'If you think that is
my bosom that captivated the girl that made her
want to sleep with me, she got sadly disappointed
injoying it, for I had my back towards all night and
my night dress was butten up so she could not get
to my bosom.'

The correspondence continued for sixteen years
and only ended when Addie died at just twenty-
eight years old. Their relationship is significant
for several reasons. Not only is it rare that we have

---

1 How to turn a lesbian on – ask for consent.

physical evidence of sex and love between two women during the American Civil War, but also, they were Black and came from very different backgrounds, Addie working-class and Rebecca well-educated. It's also great to see a woman attempting to make another woman jealous, using the same tactics that many lesbians use today. *Perhaps I will give my consent one of these nights?* In other words, 'I'm gonna shag someone else if you don't reassure me of your feelings'.

()

Civil wars were seemingly contagious, because in 1936, Spain's right-wing nationalists went head-to-head with the left-wing democrats. The war ended in favour of the nationalists, but the left didn't go down easily, just ask Lucía Sánchez Saornil. Well, you can't because she's dead, but you know what I mean.

Lucía was born in Madrid in 1895. Unlike many women at the time, Lucía was educated and attended the Royal Academy of Fine Arts of San Fernando. She was also a writer, and during the Spanish Civil War, she made sure to write about the women who were playing their part.

Although it may sound like she was a feminist, she did not identify as such. Lucía believed feminism was for upper-class snobs who wanted equality for wealthy women and not the working class. Instead, Lucía embraced militant anarchy, fought against fixed gender roles, and even helped create the Mujeres Libres (Free Women), an organisation that addressed sexism, women's liberation and the social revolution. Oh, and she was also super gay.

In 1937, Lucía met América Barrosa. The two forged a lifelong relationship and were forced to flee once the nationalists took power.

Berlin: queer oasis

In 1933, Adolf Hitler was elected chancellor of Germany and immediately acted like a dick. Before Hitler, 1920s Berlin was heaving with homos. It wasn't quite legal, but queers were tolerated as religion was rejected in favour of more progressive attitudes towards sex and gender. The homosexuals embraced this relaxed attitude and started calling their gay bars super gay names like Dorian Gray and The Magic Flute Dance Palace. The best thing of all? It wasn't just queer men; queer women were also invited to the party. Finally!

One of these women was Lotte Hahm. Lotte owned Violetta, the most successful women-only club in Berlin. She was also deeply entrenched in the lesbian scene and wrote for the lesbian-themed magazine *Die Freundin* (The Girlfriend).

Not long after Hitler was elected, Violetta was closed, same-sex dancing was banned, and on 8 March 1933, the last issue of *Die Freundin* was published. Then, one day, while Lotte was out walking, a random man appeared from nowhere and asked her to watch his suitcase. Before she could say anything, the man had vanished, and the Gestapo were emptying the bag's contents onto the ground. Lotte watched in horror as communist paraphernalia fell from the bag and scattered across the ground.

Lotte was arrested and sent to Moringen, a concentration camp for women. Once there she was beaten, whipped and thrown into ice-cold baths, an experience that left her half-paralysed. After a visit from Heinrich Himmler, the camp was closed, and Lotte was one of just a select few who were miraculously released back to Berlin. When she arrived, she resumed organising underground social events for lesbians and did so until her death in 1967.

But Lotte Hahm wasn't the only luscious lesbian in town. Berlin was also home to the comedy queen Claire Waldoff. Claire was known for her fast-paced wit, double-entendres and extreme sass, which she showcased at her successful cabaret show. At the same time, Claire's girlfriend, Olga 'Olly' von Roeder, ran a popular salon that she held in their home. The salon attracted entertainers from all over Berlin, including Marlene Dietrich; no surprises there then. Claire and Olly were very smitten, so smitten that Claire later said, 'We both hit the jackpot with each other… Olly is a truly rare, honourable character, a wonderful person.'

They were #lesbiangoals.

The Nazis didn't like Claire and Olly, or their band of merry lesbians, so they closed her show and told everyone that she had killed herself. She hadn't. So, after providing the Nazis with her Aryan certificate (yep, that was a thing) Claire was once more allowed to perform. It didn't last long, though, since Claire's raunchy songs, and the Jews who composed them, continued to irritate the Nazis. She was banned yet again.

Unlike many, Claire and Olly were lucky enough to move to Bavaria and live a relatively peaceful life. They died within five years of one another (Claire in 1957 and Olly in 1963) and were buried on the same lot.

Berlin wasn't the only place embracing sexual liberation before the war. Paris also enjoyed a little slap and tickle. Le Monocle, one of the hottest clubs in town, welcomed all sorts of identities and capitalised on breaking gender boundaries.

It was also run by the glamorously groomed Lulu de Montparnasse, a beautiful butch with a slick haircut and a superbly tailored tuxedo. The club became so popular that women came from far and wide to experience the wonders inside.

It was named after a trend at the time where *certain* women wore a monocle to discreetly let others know that they were into puss. Soon enough, the monocle became part of the lesbian uniform, the Birkenstock of its day, and a must-have in a lesbian wardrobe. Le Monocle thrived throughout the 1920s and 1930s, but of course, after the Nazis occupied France, it was closed.

()

Lesbians have always been great at creating spaces for themselves. Take Polish immigrant Eva Kotchever, who in 1925 opened lesbian tearoom Eve's Hangout in Greenwich Village, New York.

Eve's Hangout was everything you would expect from a Greenwich Village lesbian tearoom. There were regular poetry readings, dramatic musical presentations, intense group discussions, cat chat, sex chat and tea chat. Eva also included men, and had a sign on the door that said, 'Men are admitted but not welcome'.

And people say lesbians aren't funny?

The bar was successful, but because a successful lesbian is a threat to humanity, the police ransacked the joint. During the raid, the police found Eva's collection of lesbian-centred sexual stories. Eva tried to pretend that they weren't anything to do with lesbianism, but the book's name, *Lesbian Love*, gave it away.

Eva was arrested and charged with obscenity and disorderly conduct. She was deported back to Poland but somehow managed to make her way to France, where she opened another lesbian tearoom that was equally successful. Not long after, the Nazis invaded France. They didn't like Eva or her successful lesbian tearoom. She would be murdered along with thousands of other lesbians in Auschwitz.

Fuck fascism

In the early days of Nazi Germany, lesbianism was not against the law. The Nazis' main concern was with race, so it didn't really matter where a woman stuck her fingers, so long as she had a womb to reproduce white genes.

As the Second World War progressed, things changed, and lesbians were often arrested and sent to their deaths. For instance, Henny Schermann and Mary Punjer were murdered for drinking in an underground lesbian bar. The Nazis described Henny as a 'compulsive lesbian' and Mary as a 'very active (sassy) lesbian'. The perfect blend, if you ask me. On the back of Henny's prison photograph, it was said that both her sexual preference and her Jewishness led to her arrest.

Elli Smula and Margarete Rosenberg were arrested after their co-workers had grassed them up to the Gestapo. The Gestapo claimed that their sexual orientation had made them shit at their jobs, so they were sent to the Ravensbrück women's concentration camp with the word 'lesbian' emblazoned on their documents.

Thankfully, some lesbians *did* escape, one being Annette Eick. Before the war, Annette delighted in the Berlin queer scene, and often drank in the Dorian Gray. It was here Annette met Marlene Dietrich, or a girl who looked like her anyway. The two got chatting, started flirting, and ended up in bed. The next day, the Nazis arrived, and the Dietrich lookalike disappeared.

Annette was Jewish, *and* a lesbian, so she needed to get out of Germany ASAP. She had heard that a nearby farm was offering permits for Jewish youths, so she made her way there in the hope that she could get one. Not long after, the farm was invaded and everybody was taken to a police prison. Luckily,

Annette managed to escape, but her passport was still at the farm. Like a boss, she waited until dark, crept into the farm and recovered her passport among the debris.

On her way back home, she was stopped by a postman, who gave her a letter.

'It's a love letter,' he said.

Annette tore open the letter and found an immigration permit for England. It was from the Marlene Dietrich lookalike. Although she managed to escape, she never saw her parents again, and lived the remainder of her life in England.

Never seeing your parents again was a common consequence at the time. In 1942, thirteen-year-old Anne Frank, her family and several others went into hiding in a secret annex located in the rear end of a large building in the centre of Amsterdam. To pass the time and because she loved writing, Anne kept a day-to-day record in a diary that she had purchased just before the war. In the diary, she wrote about her relationships with her family, the other people who were sharing the annex, and her life before the war.

In 1944, the annex was raided, and the group were discovered and deported to Auschwitz. When they arrived, Anne's father, Otto Frank, was immediately separated from his wife, Edith, and his two daughters, Margot and Anne. Edith then remained at Auschwitz and starved to death, while Margot and Anne were sent to Bergen-Belsen, where they died of typhus.

Otto was rescued and liberated by Soviet troops in early 1945. Upon his release, he made his way back to Amsterdam and soon realised that out of all those taken from the annex, he was the only one who had survived. He also discovered that Anne's diary had been salvaged by a resident of the house.

The diary was eventually published, although Anne's potential queerness like her romantic feelings towards her friend Jacqueline van Maarsen were not originally included. In an entry from January 1944, finally published in 1986, Anne wrote about wanting to touch Jacque's breasts and kiss her. Female nudes sent her into ecstasy: 'Sometimes I find them so exquisite I have to struggle to hold back my tears. If only I had a girlfriend!'

Bet you don't remember that from history class.

When asked about her relationship with Anne years later, Jacqueline said, 'We had a close relationship and I liked being with her, but she laid a claim on me and I didn't know how to handle that. I always had to prove to her that we were "best friends". Her passionate declarations of friendship were too much for me sometimes. Then I met up with other friends and she was jealous and unhappy.'

Maybe Anne would have gone on to identify as lesbian. Maybe she wouldn't have. But there was no denying Anne's longing for her friend, how she missed her, and how she got excited when she thought about her. Her would-be sexual preferences are not relevant to her fame, not really. But I wish she could have known that, in different circumstances, her longing might one day be understood and even reciprocated.

The quashing of queer culture was not among the worst Nazi atrocities. While we will never know how this sub-culture would have evolved in their absence, we do know that 1920s Europe had been kind to people who did not comply with compulsory heterosexuality. Berlin had numerous bars welcoming gay, bisexual, lesbian and trans folk, as did Vienna. There was even an institute for sexual research, specialising in what we would now refer to as transgender studies, a subject that had been rarely investigated before. In Italy there were queer districts, in Paris there were queer bookshops, and even European films were beginning to portray sympathetic, even likeable queer characters. But faced with the far greater powers of Nazism and fascism, queer culture didn't have a hope in hell of flourishing.

SILLY SEXOLOGISTS

In the late nineteenth century, German psychiatrist and straight white male Karl Westphal took it upon himself to explain homosexuality. Westphal believed that psychotic behaviour was linked to homosexuality, so he wrote about it in a little essay called 'Contrary Sexual Feeling'. The paper inspired several doctors and scholars to become obsessed with sex and sexuality, thus the sexologist was born.

According to most sexologists, homosexuals (a term *they* coined) did not choose to be homosexual, and in a pre-Lady Gaga world, they were born this way. So far so good, right? No, they thought homosexuality was a medical and not a moral issue, so they advised heterosexuals to stop killing, beating or excluding homosexuals, and to just accept that they were simply, well, insane.

They also believed that men were active in their sexual desires and that women were passive little flowers with no sexual appetite whatsoever. Tell that to Anne Lister. As a result, they found it *unfathomable* that two women could have sex without a penis. When they eventually figured it out, they concluded that women who desired other women were, at their core, inverted men. 'Does this mean we get to make important decisions and speak without being interru—' Damn. The word 'invert' went viral, much like 'mansplain' or 'sexting' now, only it was incredibly offensive. German psychiatrist Richard von Krafft-Ebing thought 'inverts' were all repressed pathological men. He then kindly explained why they were repressed pathological men in the aptly named *Psychopathia Sexualis*, published in 1886. For those who are curious and would like to know if they are also repressed pathological men, here is a test based on Richard's research.

HOW MUCH OF A REPRESSED PATHOLOGICAL MAN (BUT REALLY A FEMALE INVERT) ARE YOU?

By Richard von Krafft-Ebing

If you do any of these things, give yourself a point and then add them all up at the end.

- Find pleasure in a coarse, boyish life.
- Neglect the *toilette*.
- Occasionally smoke or drink.
- Avoid perfume or cosmetics.
- Wear your hair like a man.
- Think sexual intercourse with a person of the opposite sex is unthinkable, impossible.
- Neglect the house.
- Seduce the sixty-year-old housekeeper whom your husband hired because you neglected the house.

ANSWERS:

0 Congratulations, you are heterosexual. You may continue reading inspirational quotes and listing *travel* as a hobby on your dating profile.

1–2 You have drunkenly kissed other women but only at the encouragement of men.

3–6 You have had your fingers inside a few vaginas.

7–8 You are a repressed pathological man/female invert. Bad luck!

Richard von Krafft-Ebing's psycho lesbian brainchild swiftly became a trope of lesbian representation in popular culture. For instance, the pathological lesbian usually pops up wielding a weapon while trying to take down the patriarchy: *The Hunger* (1983), *Basic Instinct* (1992), *Switchblade Romance* (2003), the list goes on. This usually results in a brutal death and the all too familiar 'bury your queers', and when they are not doing that, they are having sex with one another to titillate men. Hello, pornography.

This patriarchal nonsense and silly sexology were not just central to a Western perspective. Over in Japan, in 1911, twenty-year-old lovers Sone Sadako and Ikamura Tamae were left devastated when Sone's father arranged for her to get married. They felt the only way they could resist was to die by suicide, so they tied themselves together, filled their pockets with rocks and jumped into the sea.

The act was seen as a Japanese traditional performance called *shinjū*, which meant dying for love. Many Japanese sexologists were shocked because Sone and Ikamura were beautiful young women from respected middle-class families and *not* repressed pathological men. Blame was laid on industrial development and city growth. They said that Sone and Ikamura only crossed paths because they grew up in a densely populated city and there's no lesbianism in the countryside.

They also blamed gender segregation in prisons, textile mills, convents and nurses' quarters. They assumed that because women were spending so much time together it meant that they were also falling into bed with one another. Finally, they attributed the decline of the Japanese birth rate to the rise of lesbianism and said that if this were to continue, Japanese people would end up extinct. Dramatic much?

Meanwhile, back in Europe, sexologist (Henry) Havelock Ellis published *Sexual Inversion* in 1896, an anthropological and historical study of, you guessed it, female inverts. Havelock claimed that homosexuality was neither a sin nor a sickness, and believed that everyone had the right to their own sexual experiences. Aww, cheers, Havelock. He also thought 'inverts' were extraordinary and intelligent people. Aww. He then came up with a list of ways to recognise an 'invert' or, even better, figure out if you were one yourself.

HOW TO SPOT AN INVERT (IT COULD EVEN BE YOU)

By Henry Havelock Ellis

- Inverts are brusque and energetic.
- Inverts are straightforward and masculine.
- Inverts are not shy when in the company of men.
- Inverts like athletics.
- Inverts have a plain and ill-made face.

Henry Havelock Ellis was so obsessed with 'inverts' that he ended up marrying one! Edith Ellis was a writer and women's rights activist. Havelock included Edith in many of his case studies, at one point trying to persuade her that she wanted to be a man. He also got turned on when women urinated, which has no relevance here but was begging to be mentioned.

Havelock noted that inverts love to masturbate. You're not wrong, Havelock. Sexologist Bernard Talmey took it one step further and said that masturbation *turned* women into lesbians. He argued that the lesbian body was a hyper-sexualised version of a regular female body, and that if you were a lesbian, it was easier to make yourself orgasm. Whatever helps you sleep at night, Bernard!

Sigmund Freud also had a lot to say about this. 'How unexpected!' said no one. He argued that inverts were *inverted* (there goes the little autonomy we had) by early childhood experiences and things like war or prison. Classic Freud!

His 'research' revealed that a woman was just a man without a penis, that all a woman wanted was a penis, and that the only way for a woman to feel better about her lack of penis was to have a child with a penis. He also said that women cleaned their houses because they had dirty vaginas vaginas VAGINAS. Sorry, all the penis talk was making me sleepy. As you would expect, queer women were confused, and wondered if they were supposed to be grateful for the acknowledgement or insulted by having to listen to such drivel. Sure, they were happy that they were now being discussed academically, rather than burned alive or drowned, but being called repressed pathological men felt more like a burn than a genuine compliment.

The 'inverts' that sexologists referred to were also always middle class. In fact, it was believed that women dressing in men's clothes was something that the poor did only because they had no money for ladies' clothes. But when middle-class women dressed in men's clothes, it meant that they were obviously crazy dykes. Most European sexologists also completely ignored people of colour, because, you know, wanton racism.

Whose sexuality is it anyway?

People still disagree today about whether the sexologists invented 'the lesbian' or simply categorised an already existing identity. While some say it helped create lesbian culture, others argue that it was more damaging than anything else. Lesbians had gone from being immoral to medically insane; they were blamed for falling birth rates and told not to touch themselves. They were portrayed as brusque city dwellers who wanted their very own penis, or they were cigar-smoking, castrated, repressed patholog-ical men. And because the sexologists had made no distinction between homosexuality and transgen-derism, everything was shoved under one ungainly rainbow umbrella.

Self-proclaimed 'congenital invert' Radclyffe Hall wrote a really depressing romantic comedy about it. *The Well of Loneliness* (1928) follows the life of Stephen Gordon, who one day learns that she is an 'invert' by reading… you guessed it… Richard von Krafft-Ebing. The book is now regarded as the most famous lesbian (or perhaps trans) novel in the world, as well as the most depressing. I mean, it is called *The Well of Loneliness*, not *Bridget Jones's Lezza Diary*.

Because 1928 was not ready for a female 'invert' called Stephen, people freaked out and said that they would rather let their children drink acid than let them read the novel. Acid!!

The book eventually went to court, where it was banned for encouraging sex between women, even though the sexiest line in the entire book was, 'and that night, they were not divided'. Not exactly WAP.

Radclyffe identified as male and almost always wore men's attire. Radclyffe also had many rela-tionships with women, such as the singer Mabel

Batten (down the hatches) and Mabel's cousin, Una Vincenzo, Lady Troubridge. Talk about keeping it in the family. Radclyffe's gender fluidity illustrates that lesbian and trans histories were (and often still are) intertwined, despite perspectives to the contrary.

As being trans was still not really understood, some sexologists such as the out (ish) homosexual Edward Carpenter found themselves discussing a 'third sex'. They believed in a genetic androgynous gene which was neither male nor female. Carpenter had been influenced by the German sexologist Karl Heinrich Ulrichs, who argued that there were men with feminine souls and women with masculine souls. He gave these people the name 'Urnings', which seems to be one of the first attempts of grasping at what we now refer to as gender identity.

While this is nice and all, it still doesn't take away from the fact that homosexual and queer women were still being talked about like they weren't there. And it was still a bunch of white middle-class mostly straight men explaining why women liked women.

Many sexologists genuinely thought that they were doing good and that by creating random theories they were *supporting* the plight of queer women rather than confusing the crap out of them. Instead, it caused many queer people to hate themselves, which then morphed into severe internalised homophobia that many queers still feel today.

What's a lesbian without a little feminism?

Around the same time, women in the Western world, lesbian or not, were fed up with how society was treating them, and it was here where the first waves of feminism appeared. Because these women were campaigning for equality, the sexologists assumed that they were all 'inverts', so they wrote medical journals about how 'inverted' women in groups were scary. I mean, they're not wrong: go and spend thirty minutes at a women's football match and you'll know what they mean.

Sexologists warned that feminism turned normal women into raging lesbians. They also implied that 'inverts' were using the movement to pick up other women while pretending to be straight, that old chestnut. The heterosexuals were scared, and saw the 'inverts' as bad publicity. This resulted in many lesbians avoiding the meetings and protests, which eventually split the feminist movement.

But the separation extended far beyond sexuality; it was also divided by race and class. In the US, first-wave feminism interlocked with the abolitionist movement. However, just like with the 'inverts', most white women fighting for women's suffrage marginalised Black women and saw them as a burden. The feminist movement thus divided into white women, Black women, 'inverts' and the working class, schisms that would last well into the future.

WHAT IS AN INVERT ANYWAY?

Did you run wild as a child, did you hate your mother, fancy your brother, did you see your parents having sex and think it best to go for breasts, are you the woman or the man, denim skirt or football shirt, lesbians will only work if one's a butch and one's a girl, sex is easy, women know what they like and how to please you, *INVERT*, don't like the name, don't complain, it's *lez* or *dyke*, or even *gay*, you could always say *queer* it's up to date, flannel wear it, sports play it, lager, drink it and then pay for it, don't worry about breakups you'll be pals in a month, lesbians stay mates with those they've fucked, get a cat and say it's your kid, stop eating meat and start hating the world because lesbians love nothing more than to bitch on the poor straights who say that you're gay because you masturbate, is your labia itchy, small, large, maybe it's missing and that's why you are what you are, your clitoris is tiny that's it, or maybe because you've got no tits, it's too late to go straight, because now you're addicted, maybe you haven't met Mr Right, or a dick that you like, your fanny's too tight, you're ugly, you're pretty, you're too witty, rug muncher, muff diver, fish breath, lesbian bed death, lesbianism results when a nursing woman eats celery, now it is just getting ridiculous…

FEMINISM AND FOOTBALL

In 1881, Scottish women's rights activist Helen Graham Matthews formed the first official British female football team. Back then women playing football was so preposterous that Helen and her footie mates opted for pseudonyms to protect their identities from angry men. Henceforth, Helen Graham Matthews became... Mrs Graham.

The first official match was an international between Mrs Graham's Scottish XI and England. The newspapers were tickled, unable to see it for what it was – a game of football. They also chose to focus on what the lady players (their words) were *wearing* rather than the quality of football.

Despite the angry men, and the silly journalists (also men), a lot of people showed up to the match and even cheered when Scottish striker Lily St Clare (or Clair, as nobody bothered to check the spelling) scored the first-ever official goal in women's foot-ball. The match was a success, so Helen, sorry, 'Mrs Graham', swiftly organised another.

This time, it did not go so well. Tensions brewed as soon as the game started. People (men) could not deal with the fact that a football game with lady players was rather enjoyable. In the second half, people (men) could not deal with the fact that the lady players were also playing rather well. Enough was enough, the crowd (men) invaded the pitch, attacked the women and chased them out of the grounds.

The female football players were blamed for the attack because victim-blaming was just as common then as now. The papers scolded the players for stirring up the emotions of the fans (men) and wanted women's football to be banned. The medical 'professionals' agreed, because if women continued to play football, they would not be able to have children. And that's the only reason we exist.

In 1895, Mrs Graham and her pal Nettie Honeyball (whose pseudonym wins) founded the British Ladies' Football Club. The team had several firsts, such as the first Black female footballer in the UK, Emma Clarke. It was also the first time that lesbians all over the country were able to fully appreciate just how hot lady players looked in their football shorts. The team's biggest supporter was

Lady Florence Dixie, the youngest daughter of the Marquess of Queensberry, or in simpler terms, some noble in Scotland. Lady Florence was a big deal: not only was she a successful writer but she was also stinking rich and a big-time feminist. After talking with Nettie Honeyball, she agreed to become president of the club on the condition that the players were as passionate about football as she was. Why a movie hasn't been made about this already, I'll never know.

As expected, the team were ridiculed in the papers for being rubbish, and doctors still proclaimed that playing football was bad for the ovaries.

Nettie Honeyball was not amused. So, she hit back, saying that there was nothing funny about women's football, and that one day, in the not-so-distant future, women will be looked at differently, they may even vote, and they may even sit in Parliament. She may as well have been speaking in tongues, for even Queen Victoria thought it was mad.

So as time went on, and funds dwindled, the women's football movement disbanded and Helen, Nettie Honeyball and Lady Florence suddenly had other things to worry about… like a massive world war.

When the First World War broke out, gender roles began to shift. Men were on the front lines, so women filled workspaces that the men had left behind. One such space was in the Lancashire-based locomotive and tramcar manufacturer Dick, Kerr and Company. To improve morale, the company formed a female football team to raise money for the war effort. The team originally consisted of eleven factory workers, and was named Dick, Kerr Ladies Football Club. Don't let the Dick put you off – this was a good thing!

The team had many gifted players, but it was Lily Parr who stood out. Firstly, she was nearly six feet tall, with short, jet-black hair. Secondly, she could hit a heavy leather ball with such force that she once broke a male goalkeeper's arm. Thirdly, she always had a Woodbine cigarette between her fingers, usually when scoring one of her 900-plus career goals. Finally, she was into women, and when she found love with her co-worker Mary, she refused to hide it from her friends, colleagues and teammates. Again, this has all the ingredients for a great movie, but I suppose no men = no funding?

They see me votin'… they hatin'…

Women's suffrage was also in the air at this time, which made many people (men) nervous. One reporter thought it would be hilarious to change the word 'suffragist' to 'suffragette' in the hope that the diminutive suffix '-ette' would belittle campaigners. The plan failed, and the suffragists started saying things like, 'We are going to "Suffra-GET" the vote.'

And people say women aren't funny?

The National Union of Women's Suffrage Societies (NUWSS) and the Women's Social and Political Union (WSPU) remain two of the most famous groups dedicated to the rights of women. The two parties used different strategies to convey their message, but at the core, they had the same goal: to live on a private island full of lesbians and live happily ever after – sorry, that is *my* goal… the NUWSS and the WSPU just wanted equality.

The NUWSS was chill. They didn't like violence, and felt that their message was best expressed with words. One NUWSS member was Princess Catherine Hilda Duleep Singh, the daughter of Maharaja Duleep Singh (the last ruler of the Sikh Empire in Punjab and friend of one Queen Victoria). Before joining the NUWSS, Princess Catherine had met the German teacher and governess Lina Schäfer. The pair became romantically involved, later moved to Germany, and lived a happy life until Lina died in 1937.

By then, the Nazis were a thing, and surprisingly they didn't really like queer old Indian women, so Princess Catherine packed her bags and managed to escape before they could get their dirty hands on her. When Princess Catherine died a few years later, she requested that some of her ashes be buried with her 'friend' Lina Schäfer.

While the NUWSS was chill and non-violent, the WSPU was… not so composed. At the helm of the WSPU was Emmeline Pankhurst. Emmeline was strong-willed, smart and dead funny, so the lesbians absolutely adored her. She was also from Manchester.[1]

Emmeline encouraged the WSPU members to wreak havoc in the name of the cause. They spat on politicians and police officers, chained themselves to railings, smashed windows, set fire to post boxes, and even detonated bombs in churches. They were also arrested, beaten, sexually assaulted and imprisoned.

One of Emmeline's revolutionaries was the English composer Ethel Smyth. Ethel was open about her affairs with women and once wrote to a male friend wondering why she could not love men as passionately as she could love women. How long have you got, Ethel?

Like the lady footballers, Ethel was labelled a lady composer, because back then whatever job a woman did, the word 'lady' preceded it. She also had

---

1 Manchester! The city that produces the most gorgeous, scintillating individuals in the entire world.

the hots for Emmeline Pankhurst. Join the queue, Ethel! But the love was unrequited. She *also* had the hots for the writer Virginia Woolf, but unluckily for Ethel, Virginia was more interested in the aristocrat Vita Sackville-West (more on those two later).

Another WSPU lady lover was Annie Kenney, a working-class campaigner from the north of England. Annie had a reputation with the ladies and was known to get around. Annie's fellow suffragette and part-time lover Mary Blathwayt hated Annie's constant bed-hopping, and even mentioned it in her diary: 'Annie slept with someone else again last night… There was someone else in Annie's bed this morning.'

Annie Kenney eventually got her philandering paws on Emmeline's daughter, the commander-in-chief, Christabel Pankhurst. Christabel was a favourite among the queer suffragettes, and many were said to have fallen in love with her. Christabel was known to dabble in the lesbian dark arts, and at one point found herself in Paris among the lesbian feminist circle of Princesse Edmond de Polignac, otherwise known as Winnaretta Singer.

Winnaretta was married, to a man,[2] but the two had an arrangement which meant she could have

---

2 Only the grandson of Marie Antoinette's bit on the side, Yolande Martine Gabrielle de Polastron, Duchess of Polignac.

affairs with women while he could have affairs with men. Ethel Smyth was in love with Winnaretta but, as luck would have it, Winnaretta was not so interested in her. Ahh, Ethel, you sure know how to pick them.

()

By 1918, some women were finally allowed to vote, as long as they were over the age of thirty and met certain qualifications, as in white, straight, wealthy, and not on their periods. But also, the war was over, and the men wanted their jobs, and their football, back.

The Football Association (FA) was irked by the popularity of women's games, with members of Dick, Kerr Ladies Football Club becoming local celebrities. To right this wrong, the FA banned women's football entirely in 1921. The reason? To protect us, of course! This was accompanied by threats of prosecution for any male football club that supported a female football team.

Dick, Kerr Ladies Football Club did not care, and ended up touring the US. But women's football in the UK dwindled until the ban was finally lifted by the FA in 1971. Then, in 2019, women's football finally got the respect that it deserved, when the world came together to watch a load of women and lesbians play football on the biggest stage of all, the FIFA Women's World Cup. The tournament, held in France and won by the United States, was the all-time biggest female-only sporting event, and propelled out lesbians Megan Rapinoe, Beth Mead and Bárbara Barbosa to international stardom.

The event was so queer that United States captain Megan Rapinoe said, 'You can't win a championship without gays on your team – it's never been done before, ever. That's science, right there!' Compared to the football-makes-you-barren 'finding', I'd say we're a lot closer to the truth here. Around forty out queer players, coaches and managers took part in the 2019 FIFA Women's World Cup, compared to the 2018 FIFA Men's World Cup, where there were none.

The whole event made queer women across the world giddy with excitement. Sure, it was mostly sexual thirst, but queer visibility was soaring, with four solid weeks of really hot women running around in shorts while at the same time proving that women could play football, and some of them even went on to have children after. But then Nettie Honeyball knew that, didn't she?

Anyway, I'm jumping ahead. Let's go back to Winnaretta Singer's lesbian feminist circle, which was peppered with all sorts of fascinating and unique characters, such as the painter Romaine

Brooks. And, while Romaine and Winnaretta were romantically involved, it was actually the Ohio-born Sappho enthusiast Natalie Clifford Barney who made the biggest impact on the lesbian feminist scene at the time.

Natalie Barney's big lesbian energy

Natalie Barney was a keen writer and eventually went on to form L'Académie des Femmes, a literary salon that encouraged women to write. She was desperate to create not only a literary history for women but one that also interpreted sapphist love outside the context of abnormal behaviour. It was also a place where women could hook up with other women. In the words of Natalie Barney, 'my queerness is not a vice, is not deliberate, and harms no one.'

The salon attracted all sorts of queer people, such as Gertrude Stein, and her partner Alice B. Toklas. Gertrude often incorporated lesbian subtext into her work, and in one poem, 'Miss Furr and Miss Skeene', she uses the word 'gay' over a hundred times. Not only was it one of the first texts to employ 'gay' when describing a homosexual relationship, but it was also in relation to women!

Before Romaine Brooks, Natalie was involved with the poet Renée Vivien. It was Renée's girlfriend,

Violet Shillito, who had first introduced them (rookie move, Violet), which resulted in Renée breaking up with Violet and jumping straight into bed with Natalie. The following year Violet died of typhoid fever, which left Renée devastated. She was also pissed off because Natalie kept cheating on her. Don't hate the player, Renée, hate the game.

Natalie was unable to remain faithful, and did not understand why she should or why her partners would want her to. The relationship between Natalie and Renée ran its course, although Natalie never stopped trying to win her back.

Renée then became involved with the Baroness Hélène van Zuylen. Although the Baroness Hélène was married with two children, the pair often vacationed together and lived as if they were a married couple. However, one evening, Renée received a very suggestive letter from a Kérimé Turkhan Pasha, the wife of a Turkish diplomat. Renée wrote back and the pair soon began sending passionate letters to one another. Although Kérimé was French educated, she also lived by Islamic rules, which at the time meant that she couldn't really travel anywhere without her husband. The meetings had to be covert.

Renée was also reluctant to leave the Baroness Hélène. Sadly, Hélène wasn't quite on the same page, and left Renée for another woman. The lesbian

KIRSTY LOEHR

clique of Paris revelled in the gossip, and poor Renée was humiliated. Then, to make matters even worse, Kérimé moved to Russia with her husband and ended all contact. Are you keeping up?

Meanwhile, Natalie was getting close to Élisabeth de Gramont. The relationship was serious, so serious that Élisabeth de Gramont had Natalie sign a sort of marriage contract which bonded them together forever. Was Natalie finally settling down? Don't be daft – she was also heavily involved with the painter Romaine Brooks, remember? Try to keep up.

Both Élisabeth and Romaine tolerated Natalie's many love affairs, to an extent. Élisabeth would invite Romaine on vacation with them and the twosome (in my head) turned into a threesome.

Natalie's next serious relationship was with none other than Oscar Wilde's niece, Dolly Wilde. By then, Natalie was around fifty years old, and Dolly was in her early thirties. Like most of Natalie's relationships, Dolly hated that Natalie was a serial shagger, which resulted in many arguments. Dolly's alcohol and heroin addiction didn't much help with the paranoia either.

With the Second World War looming Natalie and Romaine Brooks ran away to Italy. Not a great choice, because when they arrived, so did the Nazis. The Nazis didn't like Natalie's big lesbian energy, nor her part-Jewish, American socialite ways, so Natalie began writing openly anti-Semitic and pro-fascist texts. It's not clear whether Natalie did this to survive or had internalised the racism herself. Perhaps a bit of both. We do know that while in Italy, she used her American citizenship to help save some of her Jewish neighbours, and that when the war was over, she went back to Paris, and continued banging every woman in sight.

As you can imagine, Natalie had a huge influence on the queer community at the time. The greatest tribute came from Radclyffe Hall, who portrayed Natalie as the salon hostess Valerie Seymour in *The Well of Loneliness*. Remember? That book about which people said they'd rather feed their children acid than have them read it? In the book, Valerie is written as an alluringly feminine yet independently masculine lesbian, giving readers a chance to look at somebody who is not ashamed of their sexuality. Plus, she's the only bloody comic relief in the entire novel.

While Natalie may have been king of the lesbians in her own circle, her sexual exploits were extremely unsettling to many heterosexuals, so much so that a group of British male MPs attempted to draw up a clause that made sexual acts between women illegal. British MPs! Can't take them anywhere.

The lesbian agenda

The British male MPs were mortified that a clause had to be drawn up in the first place, and the Earl of Malmesbury (not a pseudonym) apologised for even raising the issue at all. This from a man who probably went through a few rounds of soggy biscuit at boarding school.

But by far the worst of the bunch was MP Noel Pemberton Billing, who often came up with ludicrous homophobic conspiracy theories which were mainly about lesbians. He also wore a monocle, which is ironic seeing as lesbians used to wear monocles to get laid.

One of these ludicrous stories involved Billing's friend, the anti-homosexuality campaigner Harold Sherwood Spencer. It all started in 1918 when Sherwood Spencer revealed to Billing the alleged existence of a German 'Black Book' that was said to contain the names of thousands of British sexual perverts. He then claimed that the Germans were blackmailing those listed in the book.

Interestingly, Harold Sherwood Spencer had also just been dismissed from the army for paranoid delusional insanity, so obviously Billing believed him to be a credible and believable source...

One day, Sherwood Spencer heard about a Canadian dancer named Maud Allan. Apparently,

Maud had been raking in the big bucks dancing in a show at the Palace Theatre in London. Her dancing was so popular with the ladies that one reviewer commented on the large number of suffragettes (lesbians) in the audience.

Sherwood Spencer had heard about Maud Allan and, as expected, it infuriated him. How dare a talented lesbian encourage other lesbians to leave their homes?! So, to make himself feel better, he told Billing that Maud was a lesbian spy who was turning other women into lesbians through the power of modern dance.

Because Billing loved a lesbian conspiracy story, he believed every word, and immediately told the press. At first, no one cared because Britain was at war and the country had more important things to think about. Billing was not used to being ignored, so he published an article called 'The Cult of the Clitoris', which immediately got people's attention, because the British public were not used to seeing the word 'clitoris' in print, in their living rooms.

Maud took umbrage, so she hustled up some lawyers and sued for libel. Billing, a true narcissist, represented himself, and even thought it appropriate to have the woman with whom he had been having an affair, Eileen Villiers-Stuart, as his leading witness. It worked, because once in court, Eileen implied that she had seen the names of all the sexual perverts in the book, the name of the judge being one of them!

Billing then found out that Maud's brother had been executed for the murder of two women in San Francisco. The court decided that this must mean that Maud was a murderer too, so with that and the perverted judge, Billing was acquitted, and the charges were dropped.

Maud couldn't be arsed with England anymore; I mean, can you blame her? After the trial, she moved to the United States with her girlfriend Vera. Not long after Maud left, Eileen Villiers-Stuart was convicted of bigamy and sentenced to nine months of hard labour. She then admitted that the evidence given during the Maud Allan hearing was entirely fictional and that Harold Sherwood Spencer and Billing had made the whole thing up. No shit, Eileen.

BLOOMSBURY AND THE HARLEM RENAISSANCE

Members of London's Bloomsbury Set were everything you would expect from a bunch of white middle-class writers, artists and intellectuals. They were snobbish and they were privileged. They moaned about old Victorian values and aristocracy but had no qualms about taking Papa's allowance each month. They were the hipsters of the early 1900s, only with champagne instead of oat milk matcha lattes.

The group met every Thursday at 46 Gordon Square, Bloomsbury, a fashionable area of London with a ludicrous number of garden squares. During these meetings conversations often turned to ethics, sex, philosophy, sex, literature, sex, economics, feminism and sex. Sex seemed to be an important subject for the Bloomsbury Set, as many of them (mostly the men) ended up in each other's beds. As the poet Dorothy Parker perfectly put it, 'They lived in squares, painted in circles and loved in triangles.'

I'm mostly jealous of the squares.

By far the cleverest of the lot was the writer Virginia Woolf. Virginia was known for her early feminist ideologies, many of which she presented in her writing. In one essay, *A Room of One's Own*, Virginia highlighted just how important it was for a woman to have... a room... of her own. Of course, she was talking about intellectual freedom and financial independence, but seriously, a woman *does* need a room of her own. 'That's just, like, the rules of feminism.'[1]

The essay also explored Mary Carmichael's novel *Life's Adventure*, and the simple line, 'Chloe liked Olivia.' Virginia was buzzing. 'Sometimes women do like women,' she wrote, and maybe... just maybe... they like each other in *that* way, you know... like *that*.

Oh, it then turned out that Virginia had made the whole thing up. Mary Carmichael didn't even exist, and the 'Chloe liked Olivia' line was created by Virginia to make a point. Crafty bitch.

It was obvious from the get-go that Virginia's affections were primarily towards women. In

---

1 Gretchen Wieners, feminist icon: *Mean Girls*, 2004.

1898, at just sixteen years old, she fell for Margaret (Madge) Symonds Vaughan, the twenty-nine-year-old wife of her cousin. Oh, the older relative! We've all been there. For me it was a sexy great-aunt.

Many years later, Virginia met up with Madge, who was now much older and had turned into a bore. Virginia couldn't believe that this was the woman who at one time had made her so hot and bothered. Later that day she reflected on her theatrical teenage thirst in her diary: 'And this was the woman I adored! I see myself now standing in the night nursery at Hyde Park Gate, washing my hands, & saying to myself "At this moment she is actually under this roof."'

Madge may have grown tiresome, but she made such an impression on Virginia that she appeared years later in the form of Sally Seton, the blatant lesbian in Virginia's most famous novel (and let's be honest, easiest to wrap your head around), *Mrs Dalloway*. In one scene, the main character, Clarissa Dalloway, fondly looks back on her relationship with Sally: 'she could remember standing in her bedroom at the top of the house holding the hot-water can in her hands and saying aloud, "She is beneath this roof... She is beneath this roof!"'

After Madge came Violet Dickinson, a family friend who was over six feet tall and, in Virginia's eyes, the sexiest thing since discovering Greek and

Latin in her father's library. Virginia had better luck with Violet, mainly because Violet wasn't married to her cousin.

The pair wrote many saucy letters to one another. In one correspondence, Virginia alluded to passions between the sheets: 'It is astonishing what depths – what volcano depths – your finger has stirred.'

You know what they say about tall women… tall fing…

Virginia and Violet even holidayed together in the famously unromantic cities of Florence, Venice and Paris, and in one letter, years later, Virginia wrote, 'yes I remember all kinds of scenes with you – at Hyde Park Gate up in my room. One of these days I shall write about them.'

Sadly, to the frustrations of lesbians worldwide, Virginia never did write about those *scenes* with Violet up in her room.

The relationship between Virginia and Violet eventually fizzled out, and Virginia met the nice but dull writer Leonard Woolf. At first, Virginia wasn't very keen on Leonard. Her sexual experiences with men were limited, and she was unsure about marriage in general. As a child, she had been sexually abused by her half-brothers, George and Gerald Duckworth, and, unsurprisingly, this had had a lasting effect on her. She also suffered greatly from mental health breakdowns and suicide attempts throughout her life.

While these factors contributed to her uncertainty about marrying Leonard, the biggest reason was that, well… she just didn't fancy him. 'As I told you brutally the other day, I feel no physical attraction in you. There are moments – when you kissed me the other day was one – when I feel no more than a rock. And yet your caring for me as you do almost overwhelms me. It is so real, and so strange…'

Ouch.

In the end, Virginia *did* marry Leonard and the marriage was a happy one based on respect and affection rather than attraction and sex. Leonard took on the role of doting husband, especially during Virginia's depressive states. A decade later, in 1922, Virginia met the author and unapologetic sapphist Vita Sackville-West. Virginia and Vita were complete opposites. Vita was a rich aristocrat and a big-time lover; Virginia was a bohemian intellectual who could cut you down in just one sentence.

At the start of their relationship, Vita mocked Virginia's dress sense: 'She dresses quite atrociously'. She also wasn't intimidated by the academic allure of the Bloomsbury Set, hilariously referring to them as 'Gloomsbury'. Look! Lesbians being funny again!

Virginia also threw a few punches and scoffed at Vita's writing: 'Vita's prose is too fluent. I've been reading it, & it makes my pen run.' Virginia's burns only continued: 'She is not clever; but abundant & fruitful', and 'I have no enormous opinion of her poetry.'

However, underneath such shadiness was a huge sexual attraction, an attraction which they acted upon at least twice. Virginia even told her sister, the painter Vanessa Bell, about their lovemaking and recounted the conversation to Vita in a letter: 'I told Nessa the story of our passion in a chemists shop the other day. "But do you really like going to bed with women" she said – taking her change. "And how'd you do it?" and so she bought her pills to take abroad, talking as loud as a parrot.'

Their romance was also charmingly chronicled in letters to one another. 'I am reduced to a thing that wants Virginia. I composed a beautiful letter to you in the sleepless nightmare hours of the night, and it has all gone: I just miss you, in a quite simple desperate human way,' said Vita. 'I have been dull; I have missed you. I do miss you. I shall miss you,' Virginia responded.

By 1927, the relationship had ended. Vita had a lot of fingers in a lot of pies and was a bit bored with Virginia. She also accused Virginia of turning their relationship into a fantasy that escaped the dreary truths of real life. Virginia denied the accusation but then wrote *Orlando*, which was literally a fantasy about Vita escaping the dreary truths of real life. Vita's son, Nigel Nicolson, later called it, 'The longest and most charming love letter in literature.'

Thankfully, like all good lesbian stereotypes, they remained the best of friends, and Virginia always had a bedroom readily decorated with fresh flowers in case Vita were to spontaneously drop by (which she often did). They also continued to affectionately write to one another until Virginia's suicide in 1941. Below is one of their final exchanges.

Friday, 30 August 1940
I've just stopped talking to you. It seems so strange. It's perfectly peaceful here – they're playing bowls – I'd just put flowers in your room. And there you sit with the bombs falling around you. What can one say – except that I love you and I've got to live through this strange quiet evening thinking of you sitting there alone.

Sunday, 1 September 1940
Oh dear, how your letter touched me this morning. I nearly dropped a tear into my poached egg. Your rare expressions of affection have always had the power to move me greatly,

and as I suppose one is a bit strung-up (mostly
sub-consciously) they now come ping against
my heart like a bullet dropping on the roof.
I love you too; you know that.

Virginia did not identify as a lesbian but, as we all
know, that doesn't mean much. It is clear from her
diaries, letters and novels that Virginia saw most
people as individuals rather than bodies limited by
their gender. She did not like labels and thought
that they excluded rather than included. Vita was
of the same opinion...

Vita Sackville-West: a celesbian

Born in 1892, Vita came from a long line of rich
nobles in big houses. One of these nobles was
her grandfather, Lionel Sackville-West, 2nd Baron
Sackville, who had had an affair with the married Spanish dancer Josefa Durán y Ortega, also
known as Pepita. The affair resulted in several
illegitimate children. Does it still count as an
'affair' if the 'affair' results in several children?
Asking for a friend.

One of the children, Victoria, was gutted that she
couldn't inherit her father's wealth on account of her
being illegitimate. To get around this she married

her first cousin, also a Lionel, who succeeded her father's (his uncle's) barony. Stay with me...

At first, the marriage between Victoria, or Lady Sackville as she was now known, and Lionel was a happy one. They had sex, got drunk, and did all the things that Barons and Baronesses do. But after a while, things turned sour. Lady Sackville kept involving herself in weird money-making schemes and Lionel copped off with an opera singer whom he later moved into the family home. That must have caused a lot of 'treble'... oh my gosh, I'm so sorry.

Amid all the chaos, Lady Sackville and Lionel *did* manage to have a child; enter another Victoria, Vita for short. Vita was a smarty pants, and by the time she was eighteen years old, she had written several (unpublished) novels. She had also been proposed to countless times, proposals that she had rejected. For Vita was not ready for marriage, nor was she interested in men; instead she was necking school pal Rosamund Grosvenor.

The relationship between Vita and Rosamund was based purely on sex – well, for Vita anyway. Vita reflected on the relationship years later: 'my liaison with Rosamund was, in a sense, superficial. I mean that it was almost exclusively physical, as, to be frank, she always bored me as a companion. I was very fond of her, however; she had a sweet nature. But she was quite stupid...'

In 1910, Vita met diplomat Harold Nicolson. Harold proposed and Vita accepted even though she was still sleeping with Rosamund. Again, Vita reflected on the decision years later: 'It never struck me as wrong that I should be more or less engaged to Harold, and at the same time much in love with Rosamund. The fact is that I regarded Harold far more as a playfellow than in any other light. Our relationship was so fresh, so intellectual, so unphysical, that I never thought of him in that aspect at all.'

Vita wasn't bothered about the wedding and later called it 'the same for everybody'. I mean, she's not wrong. Vita's mother, Lady Sackville, also wasn't bothered, and opted to stay in bed because she didn't want to be emotional.[2]

Rosamund *did* care, especially as Vita had insensitively asked her to be a bridesmaid. Rosamund had spent weeks leading up to the wedding bawling her eyes out and was completely heartbroken, something Vita was very aware of. There was also another notable absentee, the man the myth the legend, Vita's special friend, Violet Keppel…

Violet was the daughter of Alice Keppel, a mistress of King Edward VII. The King would casually visit the Keppel household for what he would call

---

2 Can it be said that the hot mess that is Lady Sackville is my favourite character in all of this.

'afternoon tea' – what the rest of us would call full-blown sex.

Vita first met Violet at the bedside of a friend with a broken leg. I don't know why that's funny, but it just is. Things escalated, and when Vita turned sixteen, Violet gave her a ring as a symbol of their love. The love affair came to an end when Violet learnt through someone else that Vita was engaged. The ever-obtuse Vita had struck once again and conveniently forgotten to tell her.

Vita and Harold got married and were happy. They shared a deep and emotional bond and loved each other dearly. At the same time, Vita was bedding as many women as possible and Harold was doing the exact same thing, only with men. It's all so modern!

Everything was going smoothly until Harold was forced to confess that he had contracted a venereal disease from a random man whom he had met at a country house party. Fortunately, Vita did not have the clap. I say fortunately because she was still bonking Violet, quite vigorously too. They had sex, they argued, they fell out, they made up – the usual lesbian drama. At one point they lived in France, masquerading as husband and wife, Vita as the wounded war soldier 'Julian', and Violet the loving wife. Now that's a role play I would like to be involved in.

Things soon came to a halt when Violet's mother, Alice, announced that Violet was to marry the war hero (and pitiful) Denys Trefusis. Violet was devo'd and wrote to Vita saying, 'I want you every second and every hour of the day, yet I am being slowly and inexorably tied to somebody else… Sometimes I am flooded by an agony of physical longing for you… a craving for your nearness and your touch… I try so hard to imagine your lips on mine…'

Vita was also fuming, but told Violet she could marry him so long as she didn't screw him. Violet agreed, the wedding went ahead, and Vita and Violet went back to France.

By now, Harold was livid. He thought Violet was bad for Vita and told a poor, pitiable and oblivious Denys all about Vita and Violet's sexual escapades. Harold then convinced Denys to climb into a two-seater plane and fly with him across the Channel to collect their wives. There is so much to unpack in that sentence, but I just can't be bothered.

When Harold and Denys arrived, Vita refused to leave, so Harold let slip that Denys and Violet had done the nasty… It was a true Coleen Rooney reveal.

Vita was distraught, Violet starved herself, Denys cried, and Harold was… well, Harold was busy with the Treaty of Versailles and trying to prevent another catastrophic world war, which kind of puts things into perspective. In the end, Vita returned to England to play happy families with Harold and their two sons.

It was after this that Vita met Virginia. Vita had chilled out a bit by then, and was looking for something low-key. Vita wrote to Virginia and was like, 'I have been doing something so odd, so queer, – or rather, something which though perhaps neither odd nor queer in itself, has filled me with such odd and queer sensations, – that I must write to you. (The thing, by the way, was entirely connected with you, and wild horses won't drag from me what it was.)' The *thing* was masturbating… right? Or am I failing reading comprehension again?

Virginia wrote back saying, 'Should you say, if I rang you up to ask, that you were fond of me? If I saw you would you kiss me? If I were in bed would you—'

The relationship may have been chill, but that's not to say that it didn't have its problems. Virginia made no secret of her mental health struggles, and Vita worried that she would break Virginia's heart. Vita wrote to Harold saying, 'I am scared to death of arousing physical feelings in her, because of the madness… I have gone to bed with her (twice), but that's all.'

Vita wasn't that scared because on numerous occasions, consciously or subconsciously, she made

Virginia jealous. One time, Vita revealed to Virginia that she had also been sexing the socialite Mary Campbell. Virginia wasn't that shocked and replied, 'And ain't it wretched you care for me no longer: I always said you were a promiscuous brute – Is it a Mary again; or a Jenny this time or a Polly? Eh?'

Burn.

Vita and Harold remained happily married until Vita's death in 1962. After her death, one of her sons, Nigel, found a locked Gladstone bag that Vita had stashed away in her writing room. After slicing it open, he found a rough copy of an unpublished memoir, which he later published along with his own commentary as *Portrait of a Marriage* (1973). On one page, Vita blamed society's misunderstanding of sexuality and the concept of marriage, writing, 'I believe then that the psychology of people like myself will be a matter of interest, and I believe it will be recognized that many more people of my type do exist than under the present-day system of hypocrisy is commonly admitted.'

She finished with: 'I advance, therefore, the perfectly accepted theory that cases of dual personality do exist, in which the feminine and the masculine elements alternately preponderate... I have the object of study always to hand, in my own heart, and can gauge the extra truthfulness of what my own experience tells me.'

()

Across the pond, the Harlem Renaissance, a Black cultural explosion between 1910 and 1930 in New York City, was in full swing. The movement embraced literary, musical, theatrical and artistic talent, aiming to break free from damaging and reductive representations of Black people and culture by white media. It was also incredibly gay... for men... because even a gay revolution can entirely exclude women! Queer women *did* exist, because in 1925, blues legend Gertrude 'Ma' Rainey was arrested for having an orgy with a bunch of chorus girls. That's something to put on the bucket list. The incident was said to have influenced the song 'Prove It on Me Blues', and the memorable lyrics, 'Went out last night with a crowd of my friends. They must've been women, 'cause I don't like no men.' Ma Rainey's protégé and sometime lover, Bessie Smith, also liked to sing about girls. She sang George Hannah's 'The Boy in the Boat' (also a euphemism for clitoris), which contained the lyrics, 'When you see two women walking hand in hand, just look 'em over and try to understand: They'll go to those parties, have their lights down low – only those parties where women can go.'

Those parties with the lights down low sound a lot like Ma Rainey's orgies...

Bessie also liked chorus girls, especially Lillian Simpson. The two had an intense relationship, and after one argument, Bessie yelled, 'I got twelve women on this show and I can have one every night if I want it.' Lillian then attempted suicide by barricading herself in her hotel room and filling it up with gas. Note to self: don't tell women that you can have anyone you want.

Harlem's most famous gender bender

Singer and entertainer Gladys Bentley was also part of the Harlem scene. Like Ma Rainey and Bessie Smith, Gladys loved women. To prove it, she always wore a tuxedo and a top hat on stage. To prove it again, she openly flirted with female audience members by telling them all about her sexual adventures with other women. To prove it *again*, she married a woman in an illegal civil ceremony. That ought to do it.

Despite an open attitude to her sexuality on the outside, Gladys was struggling on the inside and spent most of her life trying to figure out why she was attracted to women. She concluded that it was probably because her mother had initially wanted a son. She then wondered if that was why she felt more comfortable in a tuxedo and why she fancied her female teacher at school.[3] When you don't exist in history nor see yourself in society it can be difficult to envision a place for yourself in the present.

When the Harlem Renaissance came to an end, Gladys moved to California and ended up performing in one of the first lesbian bars in San Francisco, Mona's 440 Club. Mona's was a place where lesbians from all over the country rubbed elbows (ahem) and the beautiful female bar staff served drinks while wearing tuxedos. Hmmm, maybe the tuxedo maketh the lesbian after all!

During this time, the House Un-American Activities Committee was, unfortunately, a thing. The committee investigated and attacked people who, according to them, were Un-American. So, what's Un-American, you might ask? Well, Hollywood, commies, queers, women who wanted careers, people who weren't racist – you know, the usual. Gladys was on their list, because… she wore a tuxedo, and at that time, female performers had to apply for a licence to wear men's clothes. There was also the small issue of her illegally marrying a woman…

---

3 Just to be clear, this *isn't* how lesbians are made, but I definitely feel more comfortable in a tuxedo, and I definitely fancied many, if not all, of the female teachers at my school. Wait a minute…

The investigation scared Gladys so much that she was brainwashed into believing that she had cured herself by taking female hormones; she also wrote an article for a magazine declaring, 'I am a woman, again.' Gladys then took off her tuxedo and put on a dress – nooooooooooo. She also married a man, which is less of a tragedy than ditching the tuxedo. Sadly, shit like this was an all-too-common occurrence; take Angelina Weld Grimké, for example.

Angelina who? Exactly

Angelina was a teacher, a critic, a biographer, a poet, a playwright and a forerunner of the Harlem Renaissance. Despite such genius, Angelina failed (and still fails) to get the recognition that she deserved.

There are many reasons for this, the first being her gender. Women weren't respected back then (unlike now…), so her brilliance was disregarded a lot of the time. The second thing was her skin colour. Black people were treated inhumanely back then (unlike now…), so her brilliance was disregarded a lot of the time. The final thing was her attraction to women. She was queer. She was a queer Black woman, a woman who was Black who was queer. So, her brilliance was… you get the picture.

Angelina came from a background of white abolitionists, enslavers and enslaved people. Her great-aunt and namesake was the white abolitionist and suffragette Angelina Emily Grimké Weld; her father, Archibald Henry Grimké, was the son of a white enslaver and a Black enslaved woman; and her mother, Sarah Stanley, who left when Angelina was young, was from a middle-class white family. It was this and the absence of her mother that influenced the style and content of her writing. But Angelina also had other things to write about… lesbian things…

In 1896, at just sixteen years old, Angelina wrote a letter: 'I know you are too young now to become my wife, but I hope, darling, that in a few years you will come to me and be my love, my wife! How my brain whirls, how my pulse leaps with joy and madness when I think of these two words, "my wife".'

The letter was addressed to Mamie, but Angelina had two Mamies in her life: her sweetheart, Mary 'Mamie' Burrill, and her other sweetheart, Mary 'Mamie' Edith Karn. Two sweethearts called Mamie, what are the chances? High, I'm told, seeing as it was the late 1800s and everybody was called Mary.

KIRSTY LOEHR

Angelina liked writing about women not called Mary too. In her poem 'Caprichosa', Angelina wrote about her love for all the ladies alongside being unable to act on her feelings.

> Little lady coyly shy
> With deep shadows in each eye
> Cast by lashes soft and long,
> Tender lips just bowed for song,
> And I oft have dreamed the bliss
> Of the nectar in one kiss…

Angelina's father, Archibald, also influenced her work. Archibald was an activist for Black rights and one of the national vice-presidents of the National Association for the Advancement of Colored People (NAACP). As a result, Angelina's writing often highlighted racial injustice and the psychological effect it had (and still has) on the Black community.

In 1916, Angelina wrote the play *Rachel* after the NAACP had asked Black writers to respond to the horrifically racist film *The Birth of a Nation*. The play was about a young Black woman so sickened by racism that she decides never to have children. For the premiere, the play's programme read, 'This is the first attempt to use the stage for race propaganda in order to enlighten the American people

136

relative to the lamentable condition of the millions of Colored citizens in this free republic.'

Writing *Rachel* made Angelina one of the first Black women to write a play about Black issues. This also made her one of the first Black queer women to write a play about Black issues.

Although Angelina was close with her father, the relationship was strained. Archibald was very demanding and set high academic standards for his daughter. Because Angelina was a boss, she attained her father's expectations, but as a result, this meant no room for exploring her sexuality.

In the poem 'To My Father Upon His Fifty-Fifth Birthday', Angelina praised her father for raising her without her mother. It's nice and all, but then she insinuates what she might have been without him...

> What were I, father dear, without thy help?
> I turn my eyes away before the figure and
> Rejoice; and yet your loving hands have moulded me;
> No credit, father dear, is due to me; 'twas you

What would you have been without your father's help? A big old lezza.

After her father's death in 1930, Angelina moved to New York and immersed herself in the up-and-coming Harlem scene. Despite being openly queer in her writing, her father's death along with her move to New York wasn't enough to free her from the closet. She died a recluse in 1958 at the age of seventy-eight.

Happy endings rarely exist in the history of queer women. You stand a better chance if you're white, although even then it's a bit shit.

I'M GLAD AS HECK
THAT YOU EXIST

In the early 1950s, Lorraine Hansberry left her home in Chicago to pursue a writing career in New York City. Lorraine was talented and soon started writing for *Freedom*, a monthly newspaper run by civil rights activists Paul Robeson and Louis E. Burnham. The paper focused on Black people and Black issues, which annoyed white readers because they felt excluded. It was fine, though, because white people had countless other newspapers to read that solely focused on white people and white issues, like how to remove Black people from their neighbourhoods. That was a big white issue. *Freedom*'s motto was 'Where one is enslaved, all are in chains' and the publication often urged its readers to recognise and challenge white people nonsense such as racism, racism and rhymes with shrayshrism. Lorraine Hansberry's role was to give the newspaper a feminist perspective on Black oppression, which she showcased through her involvement with Sojourners for Truth and Justice, a Black women's human rights organisation. Lorraine had also experienced oppression when white people with their white issues attempted to remove her family from their house on the grounds that it was a white neighbourhood. Another reason why she was perfect for the job.

Around the same time, in San Francisco, Del Martin and her girlfriend Phyllis Lyon had many gay male friends but no lesbian friends. The gay male friends thought this was weird, so they introduced Del and Phyllis to their *other* lesbian friends. Let's be honest, the gay male friends obviously didn't want to hang out with Del and Phyllis anymore. Whatever the deal was, it worked, because Del, Phyllis and their newly acquainted lesbian friends quickly became Best Lesbian Friends who then made other lesbian friends which mutated into a Massive Lesbian Enterprise.

One evening, probably while out bowling, one lesbian friend announced to the group that she wanted to create a political lesbian social club. She explained that the group would aim to discuss lesbian politics, the social structure of the patriarchy, and bring more focus on going down on one another rather than just using fingers. I may have made up the last bit, but I feel like it was probably *touched* upon.

However, the biggest reason for the political lesbian social club was so that this lesbian friend could have a place to dance because, at the time, same-sex dancing was banned, and lesbians love nothing more than a slow dance. They love equality and enfranchisement too, but let's face it, an emotionally charged slow dance really is an integral part of lesbian culture.

The rest of the Massive Lesbian Enterprise agreed and elected Del as president. They then came up with a name, a name that was obscure enough *not* to attract attention from the straights but obvious enough for the lesbians to figure out. Hence, 'The Daughters of Bilitis', or DOB for short. Unfortunately, I wasn't lesbian enough to figure it out, and for those of you who feel the same way, 'Bilitis' was the name given to the fictional lesbian friend of Sappho, created by the French poet Pierre Louÿs. If you already knew that, you get ten lesbian points and a free toaster oven. If you know, you know.

The DOB were unable to promote their lesbian political club because what media outlet would want to promote lesbians? It was decided that they would have to do it themselves, so instead of handing out flyers or sticking posters on walls, they did what *Freedom* had done before them and what minorities have been doing since the beginning of time: they created their very own media outlet. Thus, *The Ladder* was born.

The lesbian thought police

While the Europeans had been bashing out lesbian magazines for some time, it took the US until 1956 to produce what was one of the first nationally distributed lesbian magazines in the country. This is unsurprising considering it also took the US until 2015 to legalise same-sex marriage. The first edition included a DOB mission statement that highlighted some of the major problems that lesbians had to deal with, such as a lack of lesbian healthcare and an absence of lesbianism from history. But, rather ironically, the DOB refused to use the word 'lesbian', and referred to themselves as 'variants' instead.

Meanwhile, back in New York, Lorraine Hansberry had married theatre producer Robert Nemiroff. Some people might suggest this was a marriage of convenience, since Lorraine had been writing to the editors of *The Ladder* telling them that she was, in fact, a massive lesbian.

DAUGHTERS OF BILITIS – PURPOSE

1. Education of the variant, with particular emphasis on the psychological and sociological aspects, to enable her to understand herself and make her adjustment to society in all its social, civic and economic implications by establishing and maintaining a library of both fiction and nonfiction on the sex deviant theme; by sponsoring public discussions on pertinent subjects to be conducted by leading members of the legal, psychiatric, religious and other professions; by advocating a mode of behaviour and dress acceptable to society.

2. Education of the public through acceptance first of the individual, leading to an eventual breakdown of erroneous conceptions, taboos and prejudices; through public discussion meetings; through dissemination of educational literature on the homosexual theme.

3. Participation in research projects by duly authorized and responsible psychologists, sociologists and other such experts directed towards further knowledge of the homosexual.

4. Investigation of the penal code as it pertains to the homosexual, proposal of changes to provide an equitable handling of cases involving this minority group, and promotion of these changes through due process of law in the state legislatures.

I'm glad as heck that you exist. You are obviously serious people and I feel that women, without wishing to foster any strict separatist notions, homo or hetero, indeed have a need for their own publications and organizations. Our problems, our experiences as women are profoundly unique as compared to the other half of the human race. Women, like other oppressed groups of one kind or another, have particularly had to pay a price for the intellectual impoverishment that the second-class status imposed on us for centuries created and sustained. Thus, I feel that The LADDER is a fine, elementary step in a rewarding direction...
L.H.N. (The Ladder, vol. 1, no. 8, May 1957)

Not long after her first letter, Lorraine wrote again, this time describing her inner conflict with her sexuality along with the social expectations of women and marriage. For Lorraine, this little lesbian, sorry, variant, magazine had validated her attractions to women as well as giving her the tools to process it authentically and spectacularly.

I wanted to leap into the questions raised on heterosexually married lesbians. I am one of those. How could we ever begin to guess the numbers of women who are not prepared to risk a life alien to what they have been taught all their lives to believe was their natural destiny–AND–their only expectation for ECONOMIC security?... L.N. (The Ladder, vol. 1, no. 11, August 1957)

While *The Ladder* was applauded, it was also heavily criticised. Many lesbians didn't understand why the DOB were so obsessed with having what the straights had. Did they really want to get married only to get divorced ten years down the line? Did they really want to have coordinated outfits and holiday photo albums? Did they really want Chinese characters tattooed on their backs? Surely lesbians wanted to reject heteronormativity, not join it?!

Despite the clashes, the magazine was still revolutionary in that it managed to create a community of lesbians who existed all over the US, like the wonderful, and amazing, Lorraine Hansberry.

Young, gifted and black

In 1957, Lorraine finished writing *A Raisin in the Sun*, which was to become the first Broadway play written by a Black woman, directed by a Black man and to feature a nearly all-Black cast. Lorraine then went on to become the first Black playwright and the youngest person ever to win the New York Drama Critics' Circle Award. Did you know any of that? No, you probably didn't, because history hates lesbians, Black lesbians and successful Black lesbians.

At this point, some bore throws in their unwanted two cents. You know the type, 'Who cares that she was Black? I don't see colour, I see people. I've had enough of affirmative action; everything should be about talent.' Blah Blah Blah. Maybe this person should grow up in segregated Chicago, watch their father burn out from combatting the legal challenges of white neighbours and then try writing an award-winning play about it. More difficult than it looks, right? And if Lorraine was a lesbian, she would also be the first Black lesbian to win the New York Drama Critics' Circle Award. Something, that I, along with thousands, maybe millions of others, think is worth a fucking mention.

Lorraine and her husband eventually separated, and Lorraine became increasingly involved in the underground lesbian social scene, hanging out at lesbian parties with other lesbian writers such as Louise Fitzhugh, Eve Ward and Patricia Highsmith. Most of these women were white, with Lorraine usually the only Black woman in the room. Around this time, Lorraine met Black writer and civil rights activist James Baldwin. The pair became close, and Lorraine introduced James to many of her lesbian friends, which somewhat connected her white lesbian world with her Black intellectual world.

By then, the DOB had branched out. Not only did they have regular meetings in San Francisco, but they were also meeting in New York City. Del and Phyllis had recruited lesbian activist Barbara Gittings to help establish the New York chapter, even though Barbara had earlier called the DOB name impractical, difficult to pronounce, and basically just shit. Well, she's not wrong, is she?

Barbara arranged monthly DOB meetings with guest speakers such as doctors, psychiatrists, ministers and lawyers. The guest speakers would then sympathetically share their thoughts on homosexuality while offering unwanted opinions, unwanted advice and unwanted cures. *Plus ça change!*

In the beginning, Barbara thought it was great that such smart and interesting people took the time out of their busy schedules to talk about the plight of the lesbian. But, after a while, Barbara realised that what they were saying was, in fact, utter nonsense, and soon decided that only lesbians themselves were qualified enough to talk about lesbian matters. No kidding.

In 1963, Barbara took over as *The Ladder*'s editor. Although she was grateful that such a magazine existed, she hated that they still used the word 'variant' to describe lesbians. Barbara also thought that society should be the one to change, and that it should embrace lesbians as equals rather than asking lesbians to tone down their flannel shirts, oil-stained vests and mullets.

Del and Phyllis didn't like Barbara's militant approach, and preferred that the magazine took a more apolitical stance. Boring! Barbara being Barbara decided otherwise, and made numerous changes to the magazine, like replacing the weird line drawings on the front cover with photographs of real lesbian women. Now that's progress. She also added the tagline 'A Lesbian Review' in big bold letters under the masthead.

Not long after Barbara had been made editor, Lorraine Hansberry was diagnosed with pancreatic cancer. She died at just thirty-four years old. Since then, Lorraine's sexual identity has all but disappeared, mainly thanks to her husband and his refusal to acknowledge it. Ahh, Lorraine, while you were glad as heck that *The Ladder* existed, I am glad as heck that you existed too. We all are.

In 1972, *The Ladder* changed hands again. This time with a new Barbara as editor. Again, with the names! Is this some deterministic nomenclature? Would I have got more puss if I'd been called Anne, Marie or Barbara?

Barbara Grier, like Barbara Gittings, favoured a more feminist attitude. In a bold move, she removed the word 'lesbian' from the front cover to attract more women. She also continued to move away from the assimilationist nature of Del and Phyllis and added twenty more pages dedicated to feminism and lesbian feminism. Subscriptions tripled.

This once again conflicted with Del and Phyllis's original ideology, thus leading to the dissolution of the DOB and eventually the magazine. *The Ladder* ceased publication in 1972.

Barbara Gittings carried on in her quest to address homosexuality in a more positive and supportive way. She went to libraries and second-hand bookshops, desperate to find historical lesbians who were not depressed. Good luck with that. Barbara found this very difficult, because apparently lesbians didn't exist in the past until the Lesbian Herstory Archives came along and proved otherwise.

'They lived together, ate together, slept together, and had sex with one another.'

History

'So, they were roommates?'

Historians

The Lesbian Herstory Archives were created to preserve lesbian history. The archives contained a cornucopia of letters, photographs and literature, as well as anything else big or small that proved lesbians had always been around. The collection was initially set up in co-founder Joan Nestle's New York apartment, but as the years went by, the materials multiplied, and soon it had outgrown the apartment.

Joan Nestle had grown up in New York and was well known on the lesbian scene. In the early 1970s, she met Mabel Hampton, who had moved to Harlem in New York after losing her parents at a young age. Mabel was a dancer during the Harlem Renaissance and danced in many all-Black productions. When the Harlem Renaissance faded, Mabel found work as a housekeeper for, as it happens, the family home of Joan Nestle.

The pair immediately became friends, and they worked together to help make the Lesbian Herstory Archives a success; the archive even included some of Mabel's collection of lesbian pulp fiction. Like Joan, Mabel committed to the cause and participated in every pride march that occurred during her lifetime. She was so well known in the community that she was once named the grand marshal (yes, that is a thing) of a New York City Gay Pride March, and was later given a lifetime achievement award by the National Coalition of Black Lesbians and Gays. Before her death at eighty-seven in 1989,

Mabel said, 'I, Mabel Hampton, have been a lesbian all my life, for eighty-two years, and I am proud of myself and my people. I would like all my people to be free in this country and all over the world, my gay people and my Black people.'

The Lesbian Herstory Archives is still going strong today, and was eventually moved out of Joan Nestle's apartment to a building of its own in Brooklyn. In fact, you can visit the archives and see for yourself that lesbians *did* exist in the past, and they even had lives and were… happy.

'Everybody thought, "I am the only one."'

Del Martin

Del and Phyllis remained closely involved with the lesbian community throughout their lives, and in 2004, they were among the first same-sex couples to get married in San Francisco. Unfortunately, the marriage was later deemed void by the California Supreme Court. However, four years later they married again after the California Supreme Court legalised same-sex marriage for a second time. Not confusing at all… Del died two months later, while Phyllis passed away in 2020.

Barbara Grier also continued the fight for lesbian visibility, and while working at *The Ladder* helped create the world-renowned *The Lesbian in Literature*. This was a bibliography that included a rating system for lesbian literature and is now referred to as Grier Ratings. The ratings consisted of letter scales, which represented the importance of the lesbian subjects and characters, and asterisks, which referred to *how* they were represented.

For example:

An A*** had lesbian characters with truthful and passionate portrayals.

An A (with no asterisk) had lesbian characters but bad lesbian portrayals.

B or C had lesbian subplots, but they were suppressed or coded.

Finally, and brilliantly, literature that was created solely for the male gaze was rated T for trash. And, as you would expect, there was a lot of trash.

Barbara went on to co-found the Naiad publishing house and spent the rest of her life publishing lesbian-themed books for women who weren't used to seeing themselves on paper, such as *Lesbian Nuns: Breaking Silence* (1985), which was banned in Boston and condemned by the Catholic Church. The Catholic Church doth protest too much.

Then finally, in 1970, Barbara Gittings appeared on television, along with six other out lesbians. The sapphic six were among the first out lesbians to appear on television in the United States, and not only were they showing their lesbian faces to the nation, but they were proud to do it.

Before her death in 2007, Barbara reflected on her life of activism, stating, 'As a teenager, I had to struggle alone to learn about myself and what it meant to be gay. Now for 48 years I've had the satisfaction of working with other gay people all across the country to get the bigots off our backs, to oil the closet door hinges, to change prejudiced hearts and minds, and to show that gay love is good for us and for the rest of the world too. It's hard work – but it's vital, and it's gratifying, and it's often fun!'

She's right. It really is.

WHAT A RIOT

The 1960s brought second-wave feminism and everybody got along! Different perspectives were heard and issues were discussed openly and respectfully! Or at least that's what should have happened. But the straights and gays weren't as friendly as one would have hoped. The two sides clashed as the second-wave feminists thought the lesbians hindered the cause and the lesbians thought the second-wave feminists were dicks. The fight resulted in big-time feminist Betty Friedan labelling the lesbians 'a lavender menace'.

Beware the lavender menace!

The lavender lesbian insult was a favourite for straights during the early days of the Cold War, a companion to US Senator Joseph McCarthy's witch-hunt against communists commonly known as the Red Scare.

McCarthy figured there was a meaningful link between communism and homosexuality. His ridiculous suspicion saw thousands of homosexual men and women fired from government services on the basis that they were a national security threat. McCarthy claimed homosexuals were easy to manipulate and that the communists would be able to turn them. If Sarah Paulson was a hardened communist, I know I wouldn't be able to resist, so maybe the real question is: just how hot were these commies?

The whole debacle was dubbed the Lavender Scare, and not only destroyed the lives of several homosexual men and women but also effeminate straight men, or women who dared to go to work wearing... trousers.

But why lavender? What does this purple plant normally associated with sneezing and the elderly have to do with lesbians? Well, this moreish mask of mauve goes all the way back to the times of our dearest Sappho, who used the colour to describe her female frolics in various violet flower beds. Lesbians soon started using violets and lavender plants to express their lesbianism, especially when wanting to catch a lady's eye. So, you can understand that the lesbian community was not best pleased when the second-wave feminists used it as a slur.

It was a shame, because second-wave feminists were doing some great work. Sure, they continued to ignore people of colour just as the first-wave feminists did before them. For example, when white feminists wanted the pill and reproductive freedom, feminists of colour agreed, but also wanted to stop other things that affected them like forced sterilisation. White feminists weren't interested in that, because not many white women were being forcibly sterilised. Plus, they were still pretty hung up on working rather than looking after the house, although the feminists of colour were like, 'We've been doing both for years!' And, yes, sure, the second-wave feminists also continued to ostracise lesbians and were worried that their association with them would hinder political change. Take the heterosexual feminist Susan Brownmiller, for instance, who attempted to get the lesbians on her side by downplaying Betty Friedan's 'lavender menace' insult and instead referring to lesbians as 'a lavender herring, perhaps, but no clear and present danger'. A herring? A herring?! What made her think that lesbians would find that funny? Fortunately, because lesbians are resourceful and famously very funny, they reclaimed the insult and used it in protest at an event held by the National

Organization for Women, of which Betty Friedan was president. The protesters all wore T-shirts with the words 'I am a Lavender Herring' and 'Lavender Menace' and took to the stage demanding representation for lesbians.

So yeah, second-wave feminists... they... um... they... well they must have helped somehow!

A political choice?

One of the most visible protesters was the civil rights activist and writer Rita Mae Brown, who went on to help create The Furies Collective, a lesbian separatist feminist group that regarded heterosexuality as the origin of oppression. The group identified as political lesbians in that they promoted the idea that sexual orientation was a politically feminist choice and a positive alternative to heterosexuality. According to the mantra of political lesbianism, you didn't even need to have sex with a woman, you just had to really hate the patriarchy.

Interestingly, Rita Mae Brown did not identify herself as a lesbian and was vocal about her views on sexuality and labels. In 2015, Rita Mae told the *Washington Post*:

I love language, I love literature, I love history, and I'm not even remotely interested in being gay. I find that one of those completely useless and confining categories. Those are definitions from our oppressors if you will. I would use them warily. I would certainly not define myself – ever – in the terms of my oppressor. If you accept these terms, you're now lumped in a group. Now, you may need to be lumped in a group politically in order to fight that oppression; I understand that, but I don't accept it.

The bisexual community was angry too. They were unhappy with the way the lesbian community had treated them and rejected them. They were also unhappy with the way the straight community had treated them and rejected them. And they weren't the only ones. The trans community felt like they had no space within the walls of their own identity group. They were right, and even today they are still lingering in limbo, belonging to a wider community that either asks them to quietly stand at the back, or leave the room entirely.

The Latina lesbians and the Black lesbians (Salsa Soul Sisters, Mujeres Creando), the Asian lesbians (Asian Lesbians of the East Coast, Asian Pacifica Sisters) and the millions of other lesbians who also weren't white all had their own individual movements too. They were angry at the white lesbian feminists because they had made everything about them and failed to recognise all the issues entangled at the intersection of race, gender and class. This, along with a shared hatred of heteronormativity, erupted into a game-changing political statement that helped create the LGBTQIA+ movement that we see today.

A butch and a trans activist walk into a bar...

28 June 1969. The tall, dark and handsome New York stone butch Stormé DeLarverie was having a drink at the Stonewall Inn on Christopher Street in Greenwich Village, New York City. Back then, the Stonewall Inn was owned by the Mafia. It had no liquor licence, no running water and no fire exits, but it was the only bar in the city where two women could dance with one another. A slow dance trumps death by fire every time.

Because lesbianism was still rather unclear, and unlawful, it meant that cross-dressing was against the rules, so when a woman was caught *not* wearing at least three items of 'female' clothing like a dress, a skirt or two pairs of socks stuffed into a bra, she was arrested. These laws technically did not exist and were instead institutionalised in an extremely homophobic police institution that was prominent throughout the United States, especially New York. Not that it makes any of this any better.

At 1.30 a.m., the Stonewall Inn was raided by the police.

Stormé DeLarverie was, by this point, totally over it. She refused to leave, which inspired others to do the same. The police knew that they were outnumbered, so they instructed some people to go home. One of the officers tried to force Stormé into a waiting police wagon outside and hit her on the head with his baton. Stormé responded by punching him in the face, turning to the sea of onlookers who had gathered outside, and screaming, 'Why don't you guys do something?!'

This wasn't the first time that the community had risen, especially in the United States. For instance, in 1959, gays, lesbians, bisexuals, drag queens and trans men and women all fought with the authorities at Cooper Do-nuts, a queer hangout in LA that was often subjected to police harassment. When the police arrived for another homophobic battering, the customers had had enough and retaliated by showering them with coffee cups and doughnuts.

Queer activists had been protesting for years. But there was something about the Stonewall Riots that was different. It was a decisive moment in history rather than a starting point, and the injuries to police officers far outweighed the injuries to the community. The community had fought back with fists and Molotov cocktails rather than coffee cups and doughnuts, and, even better, the police were shook.

Marsha P. Johnson (P for 'Pay It No Mind') and Sylvia Rivera were also there the night of the riot, although there have been various conflicting statements about the role they played. Marsha and Sylvia self-identified as drag queens as well as trans activists, and later became heavily involved in the Gay Liberation Front as well as the first Christopher Street Liberation Pride which occurred one year later to mark the anniversary of the riots. They also co-founded the Street Transvestite Action Revolutionaries organisation which provided shelter for homeless gay and trans street kids.

But even though the Stonewall Riots had brought the community together, it was still operating on a somewhat separatist philosophy that relegated drag queen/trans activists to the bottom of the ladder. As a result, Marsha and Sylvia received no help and were forced to pay the rent for the shelter with the money that they made through sex work on the street.

The gay and lesbian committee also decided to ban drag queens from their marches and parades because they said that they were giving the community a bad name. Hmm, where have we heard that before? Marsha and Sylvia ignored them and, during one of the parades, marched ahead of the other activists.

In 1992, Marsha P. Johnson's body was found floating in the Hudson River. The death was deemed a suicide, despite a dubious head wound, and several witnesses stating that they had seen Marsha being harassed by a group of thugs the same night. Sylvia Rivera refused to believe that Marsha had done it on purpose because they had earlier made a pact that when the time came, they would die together.

Stormé DeLarverie continued to be a prominent figure on the scene and in the 1980s she worked as a bouncer for numerous lesbian bars in New York. She also volunteered as a street patrol worker, referring to herself as 'the guardian of lesbians in the Village' and their very own lesbian superhero. Stormé remained a bouncer until she was eighty-five years old and passed away in 2014.

In 2015, the movie *Stonewall* was released. The writers decided to focus on a group of fictional, mostly white gay male youths, as the main characters. The Black and butch lesbian Stormé DeLarverie was absent and replaced with a married, white, closeted lesbian who shows up around an hour into the film. Black drag queen and trans activist Marsha P. Johnson's role was limited, and the Puerto Rican-Venezuelan-North American Sylvia Rivera didn't even exist. Not only are queer people being written out of heterosexual history, but out of queer history too.

Hollywood hates lesbians

This isn't new information. One example can be seen in the 1961 Hollywood movie *The Children's Hour* starring Audrey Hepburn and Shirley MacLaine. The movie was loosely based on the true story of Scottish schoolmistresses Miss Woods and Miss Pirie, who in 1811 were accused of shacking up at school. It was their students who had dobbed them into the authorities after claiming that they had seen Miss Woods climbing into bed with Miss Pirie. The students then said that the bed would shake followed by that all too familiar 'wet sound' and shrieks of 'oh, do it darling' and again, that all too familiar saying, 'oh you are in the wrong place'.

The teachers ended up losing their school and were shunned by their community. The movie followed suit, and while it certainly contained lesbian subtext, Audrey Hepburn was given a real-life husband to play with and the lesbian element was seriously frowned upon, as in, it was something that should never ever ever ever ever happen and look at all the awful and bad things that will happen to you if you choose that way of life.

Also, take Sally Miller Gearhart, whose life and work was completely erased in the Hollywood movie *Milk* (2008). This woman was the first out lesbian to obtain a tenure track faculty position at San Francisco State University. This woman helped create one of the first women and gender studies programmes in the United Sates. This woman made headlines in 1978 when she helped stop Californian politician John Briggs from removing homosexual male and female school employees from their jobs.

Sally, along with her friend Harvey Milk (the first openly gay male politician in the US), challenged Briggs to a televised debate, which Briggs accepted because he was confident that he could outsmart two highly intelligent queer people on matters that did not concern him. Ah, the self-assurance of a straight white man.

Briggs said, 'We cannot prevent child molestation, so let's cut our odds down and take out the homosexual group [of teachers] and keep in the heterosexual group.'

Sally said, 'Why take out the homosexual group when it is more than overwhelmingly true that it is the heterosexual men, I might add, that are the child molesters?'

Briggs said, 'Well, I believe that's a myth.'

Sally said, 'Ah, senator, the FBI, the National Council on Family Relations, the Santa Clara County Child Abuse and Sexual Treatment Center, and on and on and on [report this].'

When the debate was recreated for the movie, Sally failed to exist. Despite actual videotaped evidence that Sally was a human lesbian who uttered actual words in public, her lines were cut from the movie and shamelessly given to Harvey. Even *actual video footage* isn't enough to verify our contribution.

DANGEROUS WHITE FEMINISM

By the end of the 1970s, political lesbianism had become a legitimate form of enquiry, and all types of lesbians all over the world were making space for themselves within a heteronormative world. It felt like a turning point. Third-wave feminism had well and truly arrived.

One such space was the Combahee River Collective, an organisation that addressed the needs of Black women and Black lesbians. The organisation was set up by Barbara Smith and was named in honour of Harriet Tubman, who in 1863 led a campaign to free more than 750 enslaved people at the Combahee River in South Carolina. For Barbara, Harriet Tubman was a clear example of Black female collective action. For many other people, Harriet Tubman did not exist because she wasn't one of Henry VIII's wives, Florence Nightingale or Mother Teresa.

Barbara was also teaching, in her post at Emerson College, one of the first university courses in the United States to focus solely on Black female writers. Because women, especially Black women, rarely got an opportunity to produce written work, there was an obvious lack of material, so Barbara encouraged the Combahee River Collective members to bring written material (as well as their own writing) relevant to Black feminism along to their weekly meetings.

One day, not long after the Combahee River Collective was established, Barbara phoned her friend Audre Lorde. Audre was a leading member of the collective and regularly contributed her own writing. She was also an instrumental figure in the Black feminist movement and, in 1979, while at a conference at New York University, she delivered the powerful speech entitled 'The Master's Tools Will Never Dismantle the Master's House', which condemned second-wave feminism for being like most second albums: crap.

Barbara and Audre's conversation once again turned to the publishing world and the lack of material involving Black women and women of colour.

Audre said, 'We really need to do something about publishing.'

Barbara said, 'What do you have in mind?'

Audre said, 'We've got to create a press of our own.'

Barbara said, 'Yes! We need to be able to control what is published, the message, and we need to do it our way.'

Audre said, 'Yes, because white women ignore their built-in privilege of whiteness and define woman in terms of their own experience alone, then women of Color become "other", the outsider whose experience and tradition is too "alien" to comprehend.'

Barbara said, 'Let's call it Kitchen Table: Women of Color Press. The kitchen is the center of the home, where women work and talk.'

Audre said, 'That's perfect!'

Barbara and Audre recruited several other women to help form the press, such as Chicana lesbians Cherríe Moraga and Gloria Anzaldúa. Cherríe and Gloria were some of the first Chicana lesbians to talk openly about the intersections of gender, sexuality and race within Chicana culture. They also co-edited the 1981 anthology *This Bridge Called My Back: Writings by Radical Women of Color* which was released for a second time two years later via Kitchen Table: Women of Color Press. The book focused solely on the experiences of women of colour while challenging white feminists and the 'we are all in this together but first let's focus on white straight middle-class women' attitude. Contributors included Barbara Smith and Audre Lorde, along with other queer writers of colour Merle Woo, Cheryl L. Clarke, Doris Davenport, Pat Parker, and the co-founder of Gay American Indians, Barbara May Cameron. Look all of them up, now, do it, go on.

In one essay, 'Speaking in Tongues: A Letter to Third World Women Writers', Gloria Anzaldúa highlighted how important it was for women to write, especially women from developing countries. The essay also linked language with identity, a theme that the bilingual Gloria often explored. For some strange reason, Gloria didn't like that people were forced to give up their native languages to conform to society. To fight the system, she often mixed both English and Spanish in her writing and referred to it as 'linguistic terrorism'. Ahh, how I wish I had invented that term, although like many native English speakers, I only speak one language, and the word 'speak' is me being generous. Anyway, this meant that non-bilingual people were unable to understand Gloria's writing, so either they didn't bother, or they said that she was a bad writer, thus proving her point entirely. Those people were white.

Meanwhile, Audre Lorde's pal Adrienne Rich had just written 'Compulsory Heterosexuality and Lesbian Existence' (*Signs*, 1980). The essay promoted the idea that heterosexuality was an obligatory political institution, and that the only reason it was deemed 'normal' was that it benefited the patriarchy. It's true, it does!

According to Rich, being straight was just a product of forced hetero culture such as straight movies, straight advertisements and straight literature. So, all those weird things that straight people do, such as gender reveals, boat shoes, 'live, laugh, love', going to Disney World as an adult, Pandora bracelets, sending four-minute voice notes and assuming that someone will listen to the end, wearing boho dresses, and sharing photographs of their children online while hiding their children's faces but then telling their followers that if they want a photograph of their children without their faces hidden then they can privately message them as if their kids are literal fucking movie stars. So yeah, it's not even their fault, the patriarchy made them behave like bellends.

Adrienne also highlighted the erasure of lesbians and the effect that it had on lesbianism both historically and politically. She was all, 'The destruction of records and memorabilia and letters documenting the realities of lesbian existence must be taken very seriously as a means of keeping heterosexuality compulsory for women, since what has been kept from our knowledge is joy, sensuality, courage, and community, as well as guilt, self-betrayal, and pain.'

Funnily enough, this has become the lesbian version of 'live, laugh, love', and is currently hanging on some plywood in lesbian bathrooms all over the world.

While Adrienne Rich and Audre Lorde both identified as lesbian feminists, they often struggled to navigate their friendship due to their very different racial and economic backgrounds and experiences. One minute they were discussing their favourite Joan Armatrading song and the next they were logging heads over Audre's issues with white feminism and Adrienne's inability to comprehend. Although Adrienne tried to understand, she just didn't because... well, she wasn't Black. Plus, it wasn't Audre's job to educate her.

Navigating the lesbian lexicon

The integration of lesbianism, race, feminism and politics was not just central to the United States. In Mexico, Yan María Yaoyólotl Castro, Cristina Valencia and Luz María Medina had their own concerns, one of them being a lack of Mexican Marxist lesbian feminist groups. To make a point, they set up their own Mexican Marxist lesbian feminist group and called it LESBOS, because, why be ambiguous?

Yan María, Cristina and Luz visited several lesbian bars to try to recruit members. Sadly, things didn't quite go to plan after it became clear that the meetings were full of thirsty lesbians who had instead come to flirt with other women and *not* to discuss the politics of lesbian feminism.

Sadly, LESBOS eventually disbanded, so Yan María Yaoyólotl Castro and Luz María Medina went on to create OIKABETH, because, why be clear? The name came from the Mayan prayer 'Olin Ikispan Kathuntah Bebezah Thoth' (Movement of women warriors that open the way and spread flowers) and ended up launching one of the first gay pride parades in Mexico. The march was a success, and has since become a prominent feature every year.

Over in Colombia, tatiana de la tierra helped form one of the first international Latina lesbian magazines in the world. tatiana wanted to empower Latina lesbians through writing, and encouraged them to challenge social norms. For example, one of her poems, 'Ode to Unsavory Lesbians', was designed to poke fun at heteronormative societal perceptions of beauty and ugliness, which worked because it's hilarious.

ODE TO UNSAVORY LESBIANS

i love an ugly lesbian
one who walks with a limp
talks with a lisp
leaves her dentures out overnight by the bathroom
    sink
wears polyester pants and men's cologne, the cheap
    kind
has a beard so long she steps on it
sprouts warts on her toes, all twelve of them
carries a spittoon in her breast pocket
chortles at church people

tatiana also wanted to include non-heterosexual material in the school curriculum. She believed that this would help prevent homophobia in the classroom as well as educating students on the concept of identity. 'What a great idea!' said nobody, because even today it's a struggle to find anything queer on the school syllabus.

Finally, over in New Zealand, feminist Ngahuia Te Awekotuku was angry that the women's movement in her country had failed to progress any further since gaining the vote in 1893. To show how annoyed she was, Ngahuia, along with many other feminists, staged a fake funeral procession in protest.

And people say feminists aren't funny?

Not long after that, the world's worst feminist, Germaine Greer, visited New Zealand on her book tour. Ngahuia, annoyed that Germaine Greer continuously excluded Māori women, lesbians, Māori lesbians, and so on, went to the airport dressed as a witch to greet her. (I love this woman.)

The stunts were a success and kickstarted the formation of several other feminist collectives in the country. At first, the groups were full of many women from different backgrounds and cultures. But then some women started thinking that their specific fight was the most important fight, and that the other fights weren't as important as their fight, so everybody eventually separated.

Ngahuia wanted to concentrate more on Māori lesbians, Māori feminism and issues such as Māori land rights and culture. She gave interviews and talked about being a lesbian openly and unapologetically. She wrote short stories about Māori lesbians in Māori society. And at one point, she was shot at by a man because he just couldn't deal with the fact that she was a woman, a Māori woman and a Māori lesbian. The conservative feminists also didn't like her because they believed that she had put the feminist movement back fifty years rather than forward. Ngahuia didn't care and decided to visit the United States to talk more about Māori women and about sexuality. However, when she arrived, she was denied a visa because she was a Māori lesbian. Oh, come on!

But while lesbians were beginning to find a place for themselves, other members of the community were disappearing. Young healthy gay men went from strapping strong lads to walking corpses within weeks. And nobody knew why.

'Britain threatened by gay virus plague'

Mail on Sunday

HIV and AIDS 'officially' hit the United Kingdom in 1982 when popular bar manager Terrence Higgins died of AIDS-related complications. Terrence wouldn't provide the warning sign he should have because the British government was reluctant to acknowledge what was happening. It wasn't until five years after his death that the government finally launched an awareness campaign. By then it was an epidemic, and many people had died because they were not aware the virus could be passed on via sex.

In fact, British prime minister Margaret Thatcher attempted to stop public health warnings and advertisements for safer sex because she thought it would encourage curious teenagers to bone each other. Instead, this lack of crucial information ended up killing thousands of gay men. Thatcher is the person who puts their bag on the seat next to them on public transport. She is a headache that has lasted two days and shows no signs of leaving. The person who gets angry when you suggest that Elsa from *Frozen* might be a lesbian but at the same time actively ships a young woman and an *actual* beast in a movie with talking clocks and candles.[1] Thatcher's woeful misdeeds could fill a whole other book. But this is a book about forced heteronormativity and straightwashed lesbians, so let's highlight Thatcher's role in that for the time being.

Thatcher was responsible for the infamous Section 28, a clause that was designed to prohibit the promotion of homosexuality by local authorities. These local authorities included schools that were stopped from showing students that all sorts of different families existed. The reasoning for this? Take it away, Thatch: 'Children who need to be taught to respect traditional moral values are being taught that they have an inalienable right to be gay. All of those children are being cheated of a sound start to life.'

'An inalienable right to be gay' would make for some great cross-stitch wall art.

---

1 'To ship' comes from the word 'relationship' and is what teenagers use when they want two celebrities/fictional characters to hook up. Look at me I know young people things.

In the US, the Reagan administration also refused to openly discuss what was happening and even blocked funds being directed towards medical research because gay people were obviously not worth saving. It actually took a whopping five years for President Ronald Reagan to even utter the word 'AIDS' in public, but by then over five thousand people had been killed.

Ronald's wife Nancy was equally shit, because when her friend, Hollywood movie star Rock Hudson, asked her for help finding medical treatment, she refused as *that* would be inappropriate. She had obviously forgotten that she and her husband had been providing their non-diseased, white, straight Hollywood pals with fancy medical treatment from their private medical team for years. Rock later died in 1985 of AIDS-related complications.

Future President George H. W. Bush Senior was also a moron. He said in a presidential campaign debate in 1992, 'It's one of the few diseases where behavior matters. And I once called on somebody, "Well, change your behavior! If the behavior you're using is prone to cause AIDS, change the behavior!"'

AKA can everyone *please* stop being gay!

Throughout the epidemic, the media (especially in Britain) did their best to blame gay men on the basis that they were promiscuous and immoral. They plastered their front pages with the acronym GRID (Gay Related Immune Deficiency) and wrote things like, 'Britain threatened by gay virus plague'. One newspaper even had an angry vicar bellowing, 'I'd shoot my son if he had AIDS,' followed by the charming subheading, 'He would pull trigger on rest of family, too'. The article was accompanied by a picture of a man (I'm guessing the supposed vicar) pointing a shotgun at what seemed to be his gay son. And here's me thinking a man of the cloth would be a little more understanding. But we've been over this.

The papers were truly awful at the time, especially the British media. They knowingly and purposefully ignited a whirlwind of homophobia and painted the community as a cesspit of disease and sewage. What a relief the British media don't do anything like this anymore...

The lesbian blood sisters

Before the AIDS epidemic, gay men and lesbians were often at loggerheads for their political and social differences. Many lesbians resented gay men for being the 'face' of their community, believing them to be sex-crazed coke heads swanning about

KIRSTY LOEHR

in their tank tops, driven by the meat between their legs just like straight men. The feeling was mutual, with screams of 'fish' ringing through the room whenever a lesbian walked into a gay bar. It shouldn't be funny, but the idea that someone would shout 'fish' at me the moment I stepped foot in a gay bar really makes me laugh.

When AIDS came along, everything changed. Lesbians volunteered to help look after the men who had been left alone in their hospital beds to die. They watched as hundreds and hundreds of young men crawled into the hospital, only to be diagnosed with something that they had never heard of and thrown back out. In a couple of months, they would return to die or be used as guinea pigs.

To make matters worse, there was a shortage of blood because gay men had been banned from donating. But, once again, the lesbians stepped up and volunteered their services. One of these lesbians was Barbara Vick, who struck up a deal with a private San Diego blood bank that let donors designate who would receive their blood donations.[2] The San Diego Blood Sisters soon set to work, and over the next five years organised several blood drives. Barbara knew that although lesbians weren't at the forefront of the disease, they had to do

2 How many gay Barbaras can there be?

everything in their power to help those who had suffered. There was no longer a divide between gay men and lesbians; it was now an attack on the community.

But it wasn't just lesbians who got involved. Meetings to discuss the epidemic were put together by various groups throughout the community. All sorts of lives, all sorts of races, sexualities, genders; there was no time for animosity, no time for separatism, politics or agendas; everybody had a role, and everybody needed to do their part. So, they did.

To this day no apology has ever been made to the LGBTQIA+ community, and in 2016, Hillary Clinton tried praising the Reagans for their handling of the epidemic, saying, 'Because of both President and Mrs Reagan, in particular Mrs Reagan, we started a national conversation, when before nobody would talk about it, nobody wanted to do anything about it.'

Not only a huge great stinking lie, this also served to erase the thousands and thousands of activists who actually *did* talk about it while nobody was doing anything to help. Look, I like you, Hillary, really I do. You should have been president. But spare us the bullshit!

BUT IT'S OK NOW, RIGHT?

In 1985, drawing on Virginia Woolf's iconic essay *A Room of One's Own*, the cartoonist and lesbian Alison Bechdel came up with an experiment to see how women were represented in film and television. The Bechdel test, as it came to be known, had three rules.

1   It must feature at least two named women.
2   The named women must talk to each other.
3   The named women must talk about something other than men.

That sounds easy enough, right? Apparently not. The percentage *was* and still *is* shockingly low.

Of course, the Bechdel test could only be used within heteronormative narratives with heterosexual women, right? Because a movie or television show about lesbians would just be about lesbians and not lesbians talking about men, right? Wrong. Films like *Chasing Amy* (1997) failed to pass the Bechdel test because the whole thing was about a straight guy converting a lesbian, while *Kissing Jessica Stein* (2001) told everyone that being lesbian was just a phase as the main character ended up with a guy.

In the popular sitcom *Friends* (1994–2004), we got to see the first, although illegal, lesbian wedding. While we didn't get to see the two women kiss at their own wedding, we did get to see how uncomfortable it made Ross, again failing the Bechdel test. And, in the crime drama *L.A. Law* (1986–94), which, by the way, proudly announced that it would be the first American television programme to show a lesbian kiss, the writers had their characters realise that they still preferred men and so became best mates instead.

Take popular British soap opera *Brookside* (1982–2003), which made headlines in 1994 by airing the first lesbian kiss on British television before 9 p.m. Many people complained about the kiss because it was far too early to watch lesbians kissing, especially around Christmas. Unsurprisingly, the women did not end up together after the kiss, mainly because one of them had buried her father under the patio, but also because, you know, lesbians don't get happy endings. And yes, the kiss may have been revolutionary at the time, but in reality, it taught closeted lesbians that kissing another woman leads to trouble and you'll probably die off-screen.

Pink capitalism

While lesbian visibility was suddenly at an all-time high, it wasn't necessarily for the right reasons. Yes, the 1990s had brought a new kind of homophobia that meant exploiting lesbians rather than burning them, drowning them or pretending that they didn't exist. Which one's better is anyone's guess. Don't get me wrong – it was great because lesbians were no longer stuffed in the closet; but for some reason, this meant that heterosexual women soon started infiltrating queer spaces with their really annoying hen nights, work nights and girls-only nights all while giggling over their 'girl crushes' and drunkenly sticking their tongues down one another's throats because some lads might be looking.

Advertisers had also cottoned on to the fact that (male) gay couples had double the income and no children to waste it on. Sure, there were lesbian couples, but what did lesbians want to buy apart from hiking boots and fleeces? Plus, it was assumed that they didn't want manicures, they cut their own hair, and they never wore make-up. Cue fake outrage!

The newly coined 'Pink Pound' was for gay men only. And, after spending the last decade calling them plagued infectious scum, the media suddenly decided that gay men were all right. They pandered to them, put rainbow flags on bottles of alcohol and advertised watches with handsome sexy men in the hope that gay men would buy them. So, according to the media, lesbians didn't drink, nor did they know how to tell the time.

The term 'gay friendly' soon became the latest buzzword. Gay friendly? As opposed to what? Gay hateful? How is that still an acceptable expression? However, gay friendly wasn't applied to lesbians, who were instead presented as suicidal bores with crew cuts, a bad dress sense and an interest in folk music. These were real lesbians, though; television lesbians were still experimenting and going back to men.

Over in the United States, comedian Ellen DeGeneres attempted to change how lesbians were represented in her show *Ellen* (1994–98), in which *real* Ellen played a *character* called Ellen. Both *real* Ellen and *character* Ellen presented as straight until *real* Ellen came out and thought maybe her character on her television show could come out too. You know, try and capitalise on that Pink Pound?

At first, everybody thought it was great that *real* Ellen had come out and *character* Ellen had done the same thing, but when they realised that *character* Ellen would still be a lesbian in the episodes after she had come out, they panicked and complained. The network responded with parental advisory warnings at the beginning of every episode which warned parents about the lesbian content and that if their children turned lesbian as a result, it wasn't the network's fault. Ratings declined, the show was eventually cancelled, and *real* Ellen was pushed back into the closet and told to stay there until the world could figure out what to do with her. Spoiler alert: she did just fine.

Back in the UK, comedian Sandi Toksvig was dropped from a charity gig in 1994 after she had come out. It was mostly because the Queen's daughter, Princess Anne, was attending the event and the organisers didn't want Her Royal Highness to meet a lesbian. May I politely suggest Princess Anne knows what a lesbian is? I mean, she owns a mirror. Am I insinuating that Princess Anne is a lesbian? Maybe. In a family that size, someone is bound to be gay, and it's either the woman who looks like a lesbian or the man who looks gay *cough* Prince Edward.

In protest at the Sandi Toksvig sacking, the London Lesbian Avengers (yes, you read that correctly) went to the event and handed out hundreds of leaflets accusing the charity of being homophobic. The charity said sorry, and Sandi Toksvig got to present the extraordinarily British *Great British Bake Off*. What's a lesbian's favourite cake to bake? None! They prefer to eat out! But back to the London Lesbian Avengers. The group, a British extension of the original New York Lesbian Avengers, aimed to promote lesbian visibility and survival. Here are some of the things that they did.

1   Took over the Queen Victoria Monument near Buckingham Palace to protest Queen Victoria's supposed assertion that lesbians did not exist.

2   Performed an all-lesbian version of *Romeo and Juliet* in support of a headteacher who was abused by the press for not taking her students to see Shakespeare plays because they were too heterosexual.

3   Invaded the offices of the *Sunday Times* in London and handcuffed themselves to the editor's desk to protest the publication of an article that accused the London

Lesbian Avengers of hating men. *How many police officers does it take to remove handcuffed lesbians from an editor's desk? Sixty apparently.*

4 Drove around London on an open-top bus to mark the seventh anniversary of Section 28, while shouting, 'You in the brown coat, hello, we're lesbians... we can spot your homophobia' through a megaphone. I have asked before and I'll ask again, why don't people think we're funny?

It seemed that Section 28 had ruffled some lesbian feathers, because a few years earlier, another group of lesbians entered the BBC television studios calling out, 'Stop Section 28' while the extremely British television presenters were delivering the six o'clock news. Not knowing what to do with an angry group of lesbians, the extremely British television presenters just kept on reading the news while the lesbians were being manhandled in the background. Imagine being a closeted lesbian watching that live at home? I bet it was the lesbian equivalent to the moon landing.

In the music world, popular musician k. d. lang revealed to a shocked world (and a not shocked lesbian world) that she was into women. To make sure people believed her, she posed on the cover of *Vanity Fair* wearing a suit. To make sure people *really* believed her, she sat in a barber's chair and had supermodel Cindy Crawford shave her face. I'll wait while you Google.

()

So, there you go, lesbians were visible, but then they weren't. Lesbians were liked, but then they weren't. There were so many mixed messages that actual real-life lesbians had questions like, what the fuck is going on?

However, it is important to note that many Western lesbians had the luxury and privilege of being able to ask such a question. In comparison, many other lesbians around the world tended to more pressing matters. For instance, in 2009, the Ugandan government sneakily attempted to introduce an Anti-Homosexuality Bill that incorporated the death penalty as punishment. When knowledge of the bill became public, many countries openly declared that they weren't OK with what the Ugandan government was doing, so the bill was thankfully suspended.

A couple of years later, Ugandan queer activist David Kato was found bludgeoned to death in his home. David had been subjected to homophobia, discrimination and violence many times before his death, and had recently appeared on the front page of a newspaper which had listed his name, photograph and sexual orientation. The same magazine had also called for him to be executed, along with other gay men and women in the country.

David's friend, the Ugandan-born lesbian activist Naome Ruzindana, noted how the community went completely silent after David's death, and was terrified that the same thing would happen to them. Naome knew that she had to leave her home country, so she travelled to South Africa in the hope that she could integrate herself into another community of like-minded individuals.

Once in South Africa, Naome found a group of gay men, introduced herself and told them about her interests in queer politics and kissing women. The men were suspicious, so they concluded that she was probably working for the government as an undercover spy to track down homosexual men and have them arrested. She wasn't. Instead, she helped form the Coalition of African Lesbians and was accepted into the community as a result.

But, as fate would have it, the government *did* get involved, but only because it had become aware of the Coalition of African Lesbians. Naome then discovered that the government had started tracking her movements by bugging her phone and hacking into her emails. This resulted in numerous death threats which led to her being evicted from her home.

Naome concluded that she either had to leave Africa or risk being murdered like her friend David. So, she packed up her things, said goodbye to her family, and moved to Europe. To this day, Naome continues to fight for the rights of queer Africans every day.

Similarly, in China, Li Tingting made herself known to the law after setting up a Lesbian Community Training Group at her university. The group did really awful things like offering counselling services and guidance to students who had no support at home; even worse, it helped lesbians form friendships and, perish the thought, romantic relationships. The Lesbian Community Training Group was eventually shut down.

Not one to stay quiet, Li focused her energy on something else, and she, along with her activist friends, walked down a busy Beijing street dressed in wedding dresses covered in blood. The demonstration was to bring awareness to domestic violence, something both she and her mother had experienced at the hands of her father.

One evening two police officers knocked on Li's door and demanded that she open it. At first, Li refused, but after the officers threatened to break through the door, she let them in, picked up her ukulele, and played them a little song while her girlfriend watched.

When the song ended, Li and four other activists were arrested for 'picking quarrels and provoking trouble'; they were also accused of planning an upcoming anti-sexual harassment protest on public transport, which was exactly what they were going to do. While under arrest, Li and her fellow feminists were subjected to long hours of interrogation. She was called a dirty lesbian, a whore, and at one point she was accused of being a spy. I don't mean to doubt the intelligence of the Chinese police force, but surely a spy would want to remain inconspicuous rather than walking down the street in a wedding dress covered in blood?

At night, the police would wake the women up. They were relentlessly questioned while being made to scrub floors. The women still refused to speak, which wound the police up so much that they attempted to bribe their parents with job offers and lavish meals in the hope that they would spill some information that they had on their daughters. It didn't work.

After a lengthy thirty-seven days in detention, the feminist five (as they were now known) were finally freed. Li being Li, she decided to marry her girlfriend upon her release, even though marriage between two women was deemed illegal under Chinese law.

I do! I don't! I can't!

Speaking of marriage. In 2001, the Netherlands became the first country to legalise same-sex marriage, followed by Belgium in 2003, Canada and Spain in 2005, South Africa in 2006, Norway in 2008, Sweden in 2009, Argentina, Iceland and Portugal in 2010, Denmark in 2012, Brazil, Uruguay, New Zealand and France in 2013, England, Wales and Scotland in 2014, Luxembourg, the United States, Greenland, Finland and Ireland in 2015, Colombia in 2016, Malta, Australia and Germany in 2017, Austria, Taiwan and Ecuador in 2019, and Costa Rica and Switzerland in 2020. It might look good but, as of 2021, there are only thirty-two countries (out of 195) that permit women to marry other women. So, not really.

But we do have one nice story. Over in India, Geeta (an abused wife) and Manju (the local butch) locked eyes at a residential school run by a women's organisation dedicated to equality and empowerment. The two got talking, bonded and fell in love.

Geeta was like, 'I do not know what happened to me when I met Manju but I forgot my man. I forgot that I had been married. We were so attracted to each other that we immediately felt like husband and wife… After that, we did not leave each other… I knew I could lose my job. But I also knew it was impossible for me to stop… I was in the grip of magic.'

At the time, the Hindu Marriage Act allowed certain communities to define their own meaning of marriage, thus allowing Geeta and Manju to wed. Although this does not mean that same-sex marriage in India is legal or accepted, it does mean that Geeta and Manju somehow managed to find their magic.

And for heteronormativity's final act…

In 2012, Hong Kong businessperson and openly lesbian Gigi Chao was left extremely embarrassed when her dad (a self-proclaimed womaniser) publicly attempted to buy her a husband. Despite the fact she was already married… to a woman, Gigi's dad refused to acknowledge it and continued to search for suitable men at great expense.

Gigi was then forced to write an open letter to her dear dad saying, 'I'm sorry to mislead you to think I was only in a lesbian relationship because there was a shortage of good, suitable men in Hong

Kong. There are plenty of good men, they are just not for me.' She then later said, 'Since Dad thinks it's so easy for me to switch from gay to straight, I should just leave it for him to demonstrate. I think I'll marry a man when he marries a man.'

In 2018, Lauren Esposito co-founded *500 Queer Scientists*, a visibility campaign for, well, you guessed it, queer scientists. Lauren, who is one of the only female scorpion experts in the world (what do scorpions and lesbians have in common? People are disproportionately scared of them), helped form the campaign to show that lesbians can be scientists as well as deeply depressed and immoral human beings with bad haircuts.

In 2020, at the age of seventy-four, success-ful children's author Jacqueline Wilson openly acknowledged her partner in an interview. Although for Jacqueline, the topic was 'old news, even the vaguest acquaintance knows perfectly well that we are a couple'. Even better, Jacqueline finally started introducing lesbian characters into her work *and* people continued to buy her books and not burn them. That's progress, people.

Around the same time, Sarah Paulson became every lesbian's favourite lesbian when she started appearing in every movie and show on Netflix. Talk about lesbian visibility. She became even more likeable when it was revealed that she was in a relationship with the also amazing lesbian Holland Taylor. The press became focused, as it often does, on the wrong thing: Holland Taylor was a fair bit older than Sarah Paulson, hence that's all we should talk about. Meanwhile, older men have been dating young women forever.

Then in 2021, the third series of *Master of None* focused on a Black lesbian experiencing the difficulties of in vitro fertilisation and why it's so much more difficult for lesbians to have babies than for straight women. Like how if a person who happens to be a lesbian gets eaten by a whale, there is insurance. But, if a person who happens to be a lesbian wants a baby, you pay for it yourself whereas straight couples in the UK don't. It's depressing to see but the topic is barely talked about, so when you've been through something exactly the same (as in IVF; I've never been eaten by a whale), it means more than you could ever imagine.

#LESBIAN

Confidently we can now say that lesbians have always existed, even before Ellen! And, that they existed all over the world, from the UK to China, New Zealand to Mexico.

We have proven – sometimes through poetry, sometimes through science – that lesbians are as exciting, sexy and randy as everybody else. I mean, one lesbian invented the plectrum so that she could have sex *and* play the guitar, probably not at the same time, although you never quite know. Likewise, dildos have been a lesbian's best friend for... well... centuries.

It also comes as no surprise to see that so many highly educated and respected men in history were... how can I put this, a bit daft? Others were downright cruel in their wilful erasure of us.

My favourite discovery, by far, is that lesbians have always been really, really funny; a unique and dry wit that cannot be replicated anywhere else. It seems that some lesbian stereotypes are also indeed (and hilariously) true. We sure do have a lot of feelings.

We can also see that lesbian and trans communities share a valid history, despite what some people may think. And, while lesbians were and still are politically and culturally fucked, attacking other minority groups only redirects the attention away from the group that *actually* wants to undermine all others. You know… the patriarchy.

Sure, lesbianism as a 'concept' did not exist in the past, but it doesn't mean that we can't use it to refer to certain women. It's not a slur, it's not an insult, it's a word that just offers happy visibility. We must also remember that gender theory is a modern tradition, and that applying it to a society that did not function as such is just, well… like those highly educated and respected men, a bit daft.

So, while lesbians are gaining bigger platforms (yay) there is still a long way to go in terms of true representation and integrating them into the history books (boo). As I hope *this* book has shown, lesbians have fought extremely hard for visibility and acceptance, so it would be unforgivable if we were to give up the fight now. Keep including lesbians, keep celebrating women's love for other women, and keep calling your kids Ann, Anne and Barbara.

Right, I need to get laid.

ACKNOWLEDGEMENTS

Thank you to Oneworld Publications – especially to my editor Cecilia Stein – for giving me the opportunity to write about lesbians. Cecilia and her assistant Holly Knox helped make this book about lesbians a lot better than it originally was. To my mum for always encouraging me to be whoever and whatever I wanted to be. And for always making me laugh. Although, I'm still funnier than you...

To my wonderful partner, who let me retreat to the spare room and write about lesbians during those terrifying (and tiring) first three months of our baby boy's life. You really are incredible. To the Bash Street Rabble for continuously supplying lesbian jokes and for just generally being pests. To the women I've dated, thanks for the material. To the lesbians of the past, you existed, and we are grateful.

Finally, to that highly respected and 'educated' male author who told me to stop writing about lesbians. You said that being a lesbian adds no value to a story. You were wrong.

A NOTE ON SOURCES

If you fancy a more serious account of lesbian history (without sexual innuendoes and constant cussing), *Sapphistries: A Global History of Love Between Women* by Leila J. Rupp (New York University Press, 2009) is ace. Some other great sources include *No Modernism Without Lesbians* by Diana Souhami (Head of Zeus, 2020), *The Lesbian History Sourcebook: Love and sex between women in Britain from 1780 to 1970* by Alison Oram and Annmarie Turnbull (Routledge, 2001), and *Queer: A Graphic History* by Meg-John Barker, illustrated by Jules Scheele (Icon Books, 2016).

Sappho lovers should check out the first season of the podcast *Sweetbitter*, while *History is Gay* is great for stories of forgotten queers. Hildegard of Bingen's vulva drawings that were definitely and apparently *not* vulva drawings are in *Hildegard von Bingen: A Journey into the Images* by Sara Salvadori (Skira, 2019). For some hardcore lesbian action (joke) you can read *The Ladies of Llangollen: A Study in Romantic Friendship* by Elizabeth Mavor (Michael Joseph, 1971). I'm sorry, but 'romantic friendship' – what does that even mean? For some actual hardcore lesbian action, see *The Secret Diaries of Miss Anne Lister*, 2 vols, edited by Helena Whitbread (Virago, 2010, 2020).

If you want to read more (than what I provided you with) on Richard von Krafft-Ebing, Henry Havelock Ellis, Sigmund Freud, or any other silly sexologist, then please feel free to find them yourself.

There are some Natalie Barney bits in *Wild Heart: A Life* by Suzanne Rodriguez (Ecco, 2002). Or if you just fancy crying into your pillow and/or hating yourself instead, then you can read *The Well of Loneliness* by Radclyffe Hall (Penguin, 2015).

In *Love Letters: Vita and Virginia* (Vintage, 2021), not only do they talk about falling in love with each other, but they also talk about dogs, travelling, Vita's hilarious mother, as well as Vita's other girlfriends. It's a hoot! Vita's intense private memoir was published by her son Nigel Nicolson in *Portrait of a Marriage* (Weidenfeld & Nicolson, 1973). This is the one with Violet Keppel and the two-seater plane. Also, more Lady Sackville content. Virginia's diary is edited by Anne Olivier Bell (Penguin, 1985), and you can read Virginia's letters in a mighty six volumes, edited by Nigel Nicolson and Joanne Trautmann (Hogarth Press, 1975–1980). The letters contain some really funny exchanges between Virginia and Ethel Smyth and how Ethel clearly gets on Virginia's nerves.

There's more on Ma Rainey, Bessie Smith, Gladys Bentley and the Harlem Renaissance in *Bulldaggers, Pansies, and Chocolate Babies: Performance, Race, and*

Sexuality in the Harlem Renaissance by James F. Wilson (The University of Michigan Press, 2010). A photograph of the best-written letter in history from Billie Holiday to Tallulah Bankhead is included in *Lady Day: The Many Faces of Billie Holiday* by Robert O'Meally (Da Capo Press, 2000). Mercedes de Acosta's tell-all memoir is called *Here Lies the Heart* (Andre Deutsch, 1960). This is the one that *really* pissed off Greta Garbo.

For more information on the DOB check out *Different Daughters: A History of the Daughters of Bilitis and the Rise of the Lesbian Rights* by Marcia M. Gallo (Seal Press, 2007). An almost complete run of *The Ladder* is available on Internet Archive. Lorraine Hansberry's letter, signed LHN, was originally published in *The Ladder* vol. 1 no. 8 (May 1957), reprinted in *The Ladder*, vol. 1 and 2, introduced by Barbara Grier (pseudonym: Gene Damon) (Arno Press, 1975). Read about the legend that is Lorraine Hansberry in her own words in *To Be Young, Gifted and Black*, adapted by Robert Nemiroff, introduced by James Baldwin (Vintage, 1996).

If you want some groundbreaking intersectional feminist work, head to Barbara Smith's 'A Press of Our Own: Kitchen Table: Women of Color Press', *Frontiers: A Journal of Women Studies* 10, no. 3 (1989), Adrienne Rich's 'Compulsory Heterosexuality and Lesbian Existence', *Signs* 5, no. 4 (1980), and *This Bridge Called My Back, Fourth Edition: Writings by Radical Women of Color*, edited by Cherríe Moraga and Gloria Anzaldúa (State

University of New York Press; 4th edition, 2015). There's an excellent interview with Barbara Smith, amongst others, in *How We Get Free: Black Feminism and the Combahee River Collective*, edited by Keeanga-Yamahtta Taylor (Haymarket Books, 2012). You will need to Google Barbara Vick and the San Diego Blood Sisters, because nobody has written a book yet, and while you're at it, check out lesbianherstoryarchives.org and lesbianavengers.com. tatiana de la tierra's amazing 'Ode to Unsavory Lesbians' was printed in a chapbook of the same name on a single sheet of pink paper in 2004.

Lesbian in Literature: A Bibliography by Barbara Grier (Naiad Press, 1981) contains Grier's hilarious ratings on lesbian content, including the infamous T for Trash. For more Alison Bechdel there is the amazing long-running comic strip, *Dykes to Watch Out For* (1983–2008), along with *Fun Home* (2006). If you want to understand how the Bechdel test works, listen to Caitlin Durante and Jamie Loftus's podcast, *The Bechdel Cast*, which hilariously reviews movies to see if they pass (spoiler: they rarely do).

The website for Coalition of African Lesbians can be found here: cal.org.za. Founding member Naome Ruzindana also features in the documentary *Call Me Kuchu* (2012), which focuses on the LGBTQI+ community in Uganda and on the murder of David Kato.

Further sources include: *The Life and Legend of Catterina Vizzani: Sexual identity, science and sensationalism in eighteenth-century Italy and England* by Clorinda

Donato (Liverpool University Press, 2020); *The Favourite: Sarah, Duchess of Marlborough* by Ophelia Field (Hodder & Stoughton, 2002), though if you can't be arsed, then just watch *The Favourite* (2018) instead; *The Letters of Charlotte Brontë*, 3 vols, edited by Margaret Smith (Clarendon Press, 1995–2004); the unfortunately named *Beloved Sisters and Loving Friends: Letters from Rebecca Primus of Royal Oak, Maryland, and Addie Brown of Hartford, Connecticut, 1854–1868*, edited by Farah Jasmine Griffin (Knopf, 1999); *Selected Works of Angelina Weld Grimké*, edited by Carolivia Herron (Oxford University Press, 1991); *Women's Football: The Secret History* by Tim Tate (John Blake, 2016); *The History of Women's Football* by Jean Williams (Pen & Sword, 2021); an account of Maud Allan's court case is included in *Court Number One: The Old Bailey Trials that Defined Modern Britain* by Thomas Grant (John Murray, 2019); *Empty Without You: The Intimate Letters of Eleanor Roosevelt and Lorena Hickok*, edited by Rodger Streitmatter (Simon & Schuster, 1998); Anne Frank, *The Diary of a Young Girl*, edited by Mirjam Pressler and Otto Frank, translated by Susan Massotty (Penguin, 2001).